ROBOT PIONEERS

ROBOTICS IN INDUSTRY

CLAUDIA MARTIN

LUCENT PRESS

Published in 2018 by
Lucent Press, an Imprint of Greenhaven Publishing, LLC
353 3rd Avenue
Suite 255
New York, NY 10010

Produced for Lucent Press by Calcium
Editors: Sarah Eason and Harriet McGregor
Designers: Paul Myerscough and Emma DeBanks
Picture researcher: Rachel Blount

Picture credits: Cover: Shutterstock: Wi6995; Inside: Autonomous Solutions, Inc. (ASI) 22–23; Blue River Technology, Inc. 34–35; Deutsche Post DHL Group 46–47; DVIDS/Malcolm McClendon 20; Harvest Automation Inc. 40–41, 41b; Honda 16–17; Ibex Automation Ltd 42b; Microdrones ® 44b, 50, 51Copyright OC Robotics 12, 13; Courtesy of Rethink Robotics, Inc. 55t; ROBOTECH srl 32b; Serva Transport Systems 24, 25, 30–31, 30t; Shutterstock: ChameleonsEye 32–33, Hans Engbers 39b, Iakov Filimonov 5t, Fotokostic 42–43, Gaika1967 61b, Dmitry Kalinovsky 4–5, 44–45, Andrei Kholmov 1, 10–11, Modfos 38–39, Monkey Business Images 53, Jorge Moro 35r, Ndoeljindoel 14–15, Photodiem 60–61, REDXIII 18–19, Ned Snowman 59; Wikimedia Commons: Alliance Lp Drones Ltd. 49t, ASIrobots 36, Adrian Baer 54–55, Xavier Caré/ CC-BYSA 56, 57, Fick/Bruce R./Makinson/John B./General Electric Co Schenectady Handling Products Operation 15t, Gnangarra 26–27, Grendelkhan 27t, Frank Grunwald – Frankenwagen 28t, Heje 28–29, Steve Jurvetson 19, Susan Moran, Landsat 7 Science Team and USDA Agricultural Research Service 37, Frank C. Müller, Frankfurt am Main 21, Hetarllen Mumriken 52, Pzucchel 11c, KUKA Systems GmbH 6–7, Tokumeigakarinoaoshima 58, UL Digital Library 7r, Sgt. Mallory Vanderschans 23r, Richard Watt/MOD 47b, World Wide Gifts 17b; Yamaha Motor Corporation 48–49; ZenRobotics Ltd. 8–9, 9r.

Library of Congress Cataloging-in-Publication Data

Names: Martin, Claudia.
Title: Robotics in industry / Claudia Martin.
Description: New York : Lucent Press, 2018. | Series: Robot pioneers | Includes index.
Identifiers: ISBN 9781534562196 (library bound) | ISBN 9781534562202 (ebook) | ISBN 9781534563001 (paperback)
Subjects: LCSH: Robots, Industrial--Juvenile literature. | Robotics--Juvenile literature.
Classification: LCC TS191.8 M338 2018 | DDC 670.42′72--dc23

Printed in the United States of America

CPSIA compliance information: Batch #CW18KL: For further information contact Greenhaven Publishing LLC, New York, New York at 1-844-317-7404.

CHAPTER 1

ROBOTIC ARMS

A robot is a machine that can carry out a series of operations automatically. Robots are useful for doing work that is tiring, heavy, dangerous, or repetitive. For these reasons, robots are particularly suited to working in factories and other industrial settings. Today, there are more than 1.6 million industrial robots, and many of them are pioneering robotic arms.

Robotic arms are also employed on construction sites and in mines. This one is equipped with a powerful drill.

What Is a Robot?

A fully autonomous robot is one that acts independently, receiving all its instructions from its own computer, called a controller. The computer is programmed to move the robot's parts in the required ways. A program is a set of ordered instructions. For example, it might tell the robot to "move to point A," "pick up object X," "move to point B," and "put down object X." A robot does not have to be fully autonomous. Some are semiautonomous, which means they perform tasks programmed into their computer, and tasks ordered by a human operator, often by remote control.

The simplest robots are programmed to perform basic tasks over and over. They move from place to place or have moving parts, like an arm. More complex robots have sensors, which allow them to take in information, known as data, about their surroundings. The robot's computer is programmed to process this data and adjust the robot's behavior accordingly. Many robotic arms used on production lines have sensors, like cameras, which help them work with great precision. The most complex and pioneering robots also have artificial intelligence. This means they have highly complex programs that allow them to "learn" from their surroundings and from past events.

On a production line, like this one sealing and labeling bottles, a product is made by going through a series of operations. The earliest production line was in the Ford Motor Company, in 1913. Henry Ford introduced the idea of moving cars continuously past workstations, where humans were instructed to perform the same task over and over again, like screwing on wheels or joining parts together. Robotic arms are well suited to production line work, as they perform repetitive tasks without getting tired or bored. Today, many production lines are worked completely by robotic arms. Do you think there are any drawbacks to replacing humans with robotic arms? Give reasons for your answers.

A robotic arm is a programmed mechanical arm. The entire robot may be in the form of an arm, or the arm may be part of a larger robot. A robotic arm is often called a manipulator. In many ways, robotic arms are styled to function like a human arm. As in a human arm, the parts, or links, of the arm are connected by joints that allow rotational motion (turning) or linear motion (up and down, or left and right). However, robotic arms may have any number of links and joints. At the tip of the arm is the end effector, which can be likened to the human hand. The end effector can take any number of forms, from grippers to a drill. Complete with their computer controllers, industrial robotic arms can cost up to $150,000.

These Kuka robotic arms are assembling parts in a car factory. The car industry is the biggest user of robots, employing more than one-third of all industrial robots. Other industries that employ many robots are electronics, machinery, and plastics production. Why do you think these particular industries have adopted robots so widely? Give reasons for your answer.

Different forms of robotic arms are suited to different tasks. An articulated robotic arm has joints that rotate. It may have just three joints, or ten, or more. With this range of motion, articulated arms are used for tasks like assembling parts, die-casting (making metal objects by pouring molten metal into molds), and welding. Linear robots have three sliding joints at right angles to one another: one slides up–down, one slides in–out, and one slides left–right. Linear robots are often used for "pick and place" work (moving parts from one place to another). Today's robotic arms may have any combination of different types of joints to give the required movement for their programmed task.

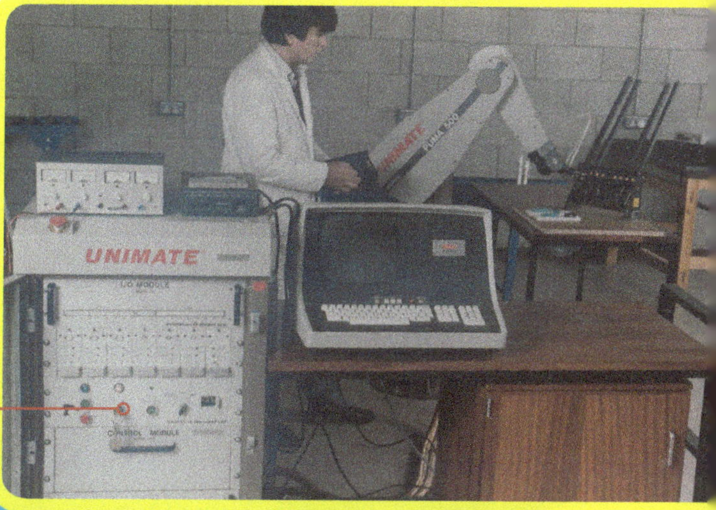

A Unimate Puma 500 robotic arm is at work here beside its bulky computer control system.

ROBOT REVOLUTION

The world's first industrial robot was called Unimate. It was invented by George Devol and was put to work in 1961, in a General Motors factory in New Jersey. Its job was to lift and stack hot pieces of metal. Unimate was the first fully programmable robotic arm. It was also the first digital robot, which, like a computer, received its instructions in the form of the digits 1 and 0. A digital machine has many tiny electronic circuits. A "1" tells a circuit to close so that electricity can flow, and a "0" stops the flow. In a computer program, all instructions are turned into a list of 1s and 0s.

Recycling Robots

Every year in the United States, more than 400 million tons (362.9 mt) of waste is recycled. The waste is collected and transported to recycling centers, where it is sorted and separated. Different types of plastic, glass, cardboard, and other materials must be processed separately. When this work is carried out by humans, waste separation is a time-consuming, messy, and dull task. When human workers get tired, they make more mistakes. The pioneering ZenRobotics Recycler system uses robotic arms, equipped with grabber end effectors, as a solution to the waste-sorting problem. The system has at least two arms, which can make up to 4,000 picks per hour. What makes the robotic system ground-breaking is that it is able to recognize different types of waste.

After it is unloaded, waste moves down a conveyor belt. Sensors continuously monitor the stream of moving waste. These sensors include visible-light cameras, metal detectors, and three-dimensional (3D) sensors to analyze the shapes of objects. Other sensors detect near infrared light. Different materials absorb near infrared light in different ways. The system's computer processes all the data, swiftly combining it to decide which material is where. Grabbers are programmed to pick up to four different materials, so the more grabbers added to the system, the wider the variety of materials that can be processed. The grabbers pick up the waste and place it in designated holders. The system is correct 98 percent of the time.

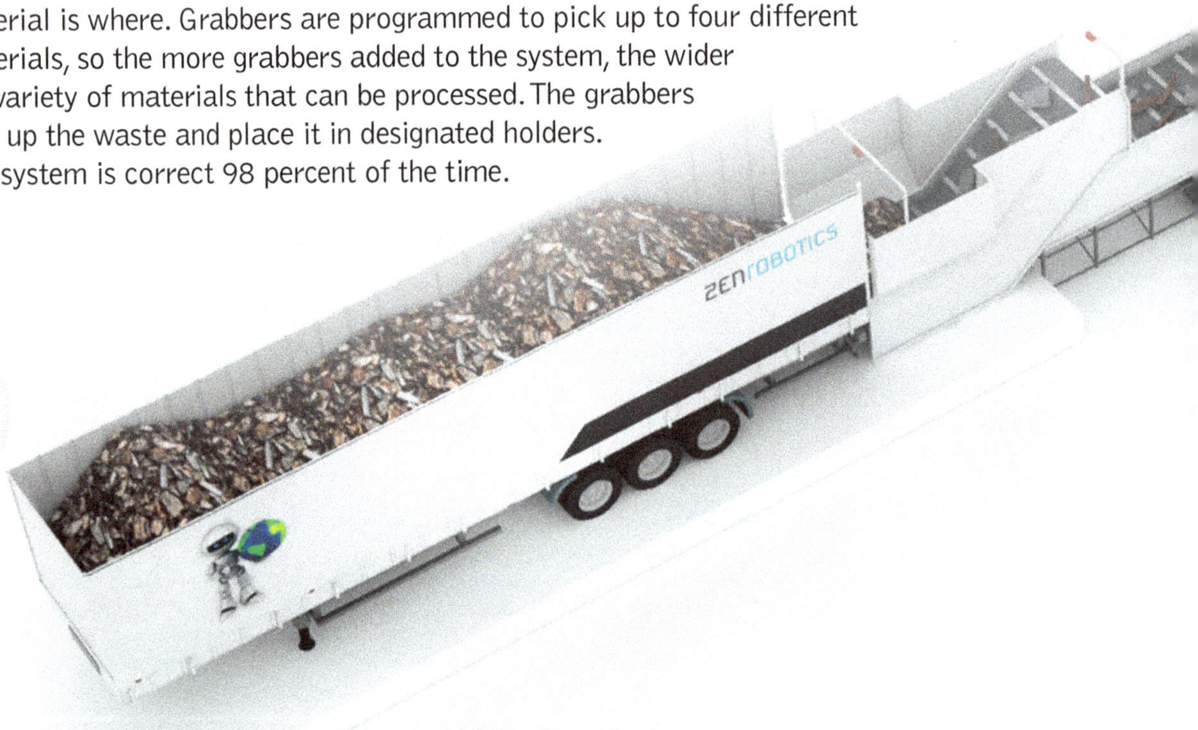

In addition to these features, the recycling robot is programmed to accept "training" from a human operator. The operator can instruct the robot to separate out a new kind of waste. For example, it could be told to separate green glass from other colors of glass. Making use of a basic artificial intelligence program, the system learns how to process the new type of waste following a training session with sample waste.

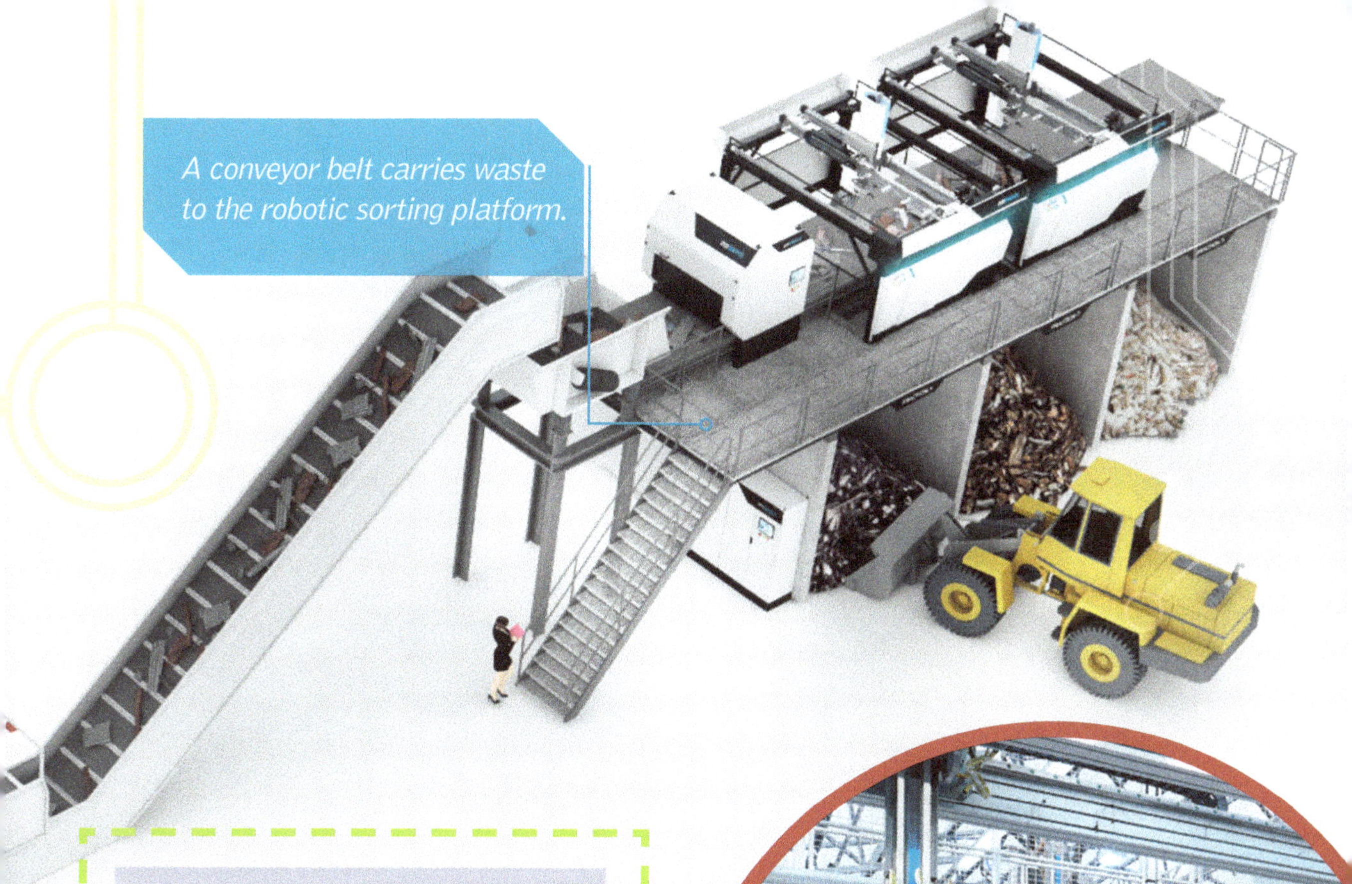

A conveyor belt carries waste to the robotic sorting platform.

The ZenRobotics Recycler grabbers are designed to pick up a wide range of sizes, shapes, and weights of waste. With the ability to open 2–20 in (5–50 cm) wide, each grabber adapts its grip for every object. Each arm can lift weights of up to 44 lb (20 kg). The pincer-like shape and ridged surfaces of the grabbers keeps objects from dropping or slipping. Each arm can fully rotate to drop waste in the correct container. Can you think of any other tasks that robotic grippers of this type could perform? Give reasons for your answers.

Depending on the required task, the end effectors of a robotic arm can be in the form of many different tools. Common tools include paint sprayers, which are usually attached to an articulated arm. They can turn and angle themselves to cover a surface evenly with paint. Other arms are equipped with grinders, welding guns, or squirters for applying glue. Some use a vacuum (sucking) tool to pick up objects instead of grippers. Multipurpose robotic arms have a tool rack and can switch between tools as necessary.

The strength, speed, reach, and accuracy of a robotic arm must also be suited to the task. In the automobile industry, most robotic arms are powerful and fast, with a reach of several feet, but they may only be accurate in their positioning to around 0.004 in (0.1 mm).

Paint sprayers are at work on a line of cars.

Sensitive Arms

In the electronics industry, in which products like computers and phones are made, the parts assembled are small and easily bent or broken. Robotic arms for electronics are typically small and positioned on a tabletop, with a reach of about 8 in (20 cm). With delicate grippers, these robots can pick up tiny parts and position them to within 0.0004 in (0.01 mm). Some grippers have sensors that allow them to change their force (the power of their movements) so that they "feel" their way through assembling a product like sensitive human fingers. To check the accuracy of the finished product, some arms are equipped only with thermal imaging sensors, which can identify heat and cold. These find hot spots, which can indicate damage to an electronic circuit.

Named Andrew, this robot works with liquid samples. It can measure and transfer exact quantities.

ROBOT REVOLUTION

The technology in robotic arms has developed to the point where highly accurate and delicate movements are possible. This allows specialist robotic arms to be used in laboratories, where they hold, pour, mix, heat, and test samples. These robots are often called auto-samplers, as they continuously provide samples for scientific testing. Today's robots can carry out these repetitive tasks very precisely, freeing up scientists for other work. Another benefit of laboratory robots is that they are able to work safely with chemicals that are hazardous to humans.

Snake-Arms

Most robotic arms cannot work easily in confined environments like pipes. Engineers at OCRobotics came up with a solution. They built snake-like robotic arms. The arms are extremely flexible, with each of the many joints able to bend in two directions. The robot's computer and its human operator remain outside the workspace, while the snake-arm wriggles into it. The snake-arm has a hollow core, so a hose can be fed through it to carry out cleaning of the pipes with a powerful jet of water. The arm can also be turned into a laser cutting tool. Laser cutting involves firing an intense beam of laser light at an object. The laser beam melts or burns away the material. The lasers are transmitted down optical fibers through the hollow center of the arm.

This OCRobotics robot is named LaserSnake. It has a laser cutting tool.

Another benefit of these pioneering snake-arm robots is that they can enter hazardous environments, like a collapsed tunnel. They can also tackle dangerous materials, such as at a nuclear power plant. If the end effector of a snake-arm robot has sensors as well as grippers, the robot's human operator can carry out inspections and testing of materials, all while keeping a safe distance. This is a form of telepresence, in which the human operator has the benefits of being "present" without being physically in the workspace. It is also possible to mount the snake-arm on a wheeled robotic platform. In this way, police officers could use it to investigate dangerous situations. For example, they could use a snake-arm robot to reach through the window of a parked car or home.

This snake-arm robot is using a jet of water to clean inside a tunnel.

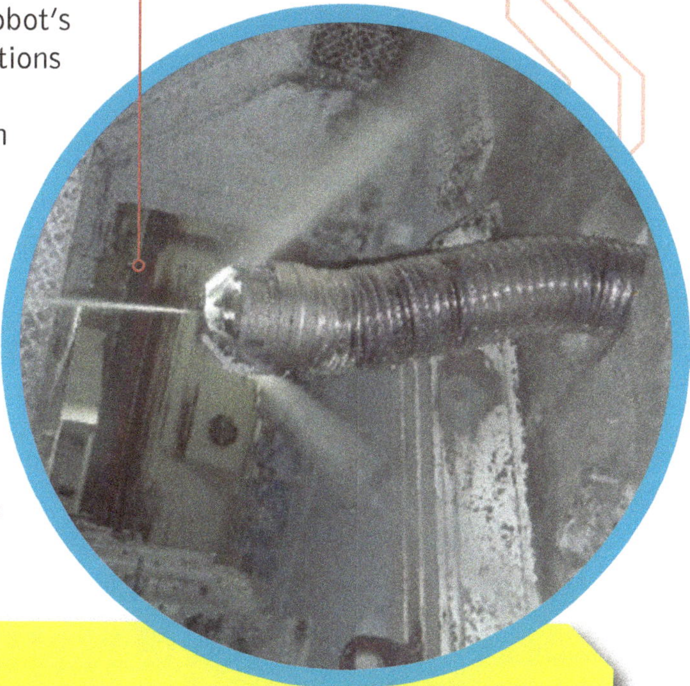

ROBOT REVOLUTION

All robots need a power source. This is usually a battery, but they may have a cable that links them to the main electricity supply instead. For the robot's arms and other parts to move, it also needs actuators. An actuator turns electrical energy into movement. If you think of a robot as a human body, the computer is the robot's brain. It controls the actuators, which are like the muscles that make the body move.

Some robot actuators are electric motors. An electric motor turns electrical energy into movement using the attracting and repelling forces of magnets. Other actuators are pneumatic. They use compressed air to create movement. Or actuators can be hydraulic, which means they use liquids to create movement. To move a hydraulic arm, the robot's controller opens a valve that leads from the liquid pump to a piston attached to the arm. The compressed liquid extends the piston, moving the arm forward.

CHAPTER 2

EXOSUITS

An exosuit, also called a powered exoskeleton, is a wearable machine that gives the user greater strength as they walk or lift heavy objects. It provides humans with extra, mechanical muscles. Truly successful exosuits have appeared only in the last few years, but one day, exosuits may be worn by most workers in industries from construction to ship-building.

Sensors in the exosuit detect the wearer's movement. This can be done in one of two ways. In the first kind of exosuit, the robot's sensors are placed on the wearer's muscles. There, they pick up on the initial contractions, or shortenings, of the wearer's muscles as they begin to move. In the second kind of suit, the sensors are placed on the wearer's skin. There, they detect the nerve signals that are sent from the brain to the muscles, telling the muscles to move. These signals "leak" faintly onto the surface of the skin. The exosuit can recognize the type of motions the wearer intends to make.

When the robot senses that the wearer is moving or about to move, actuators (robot muscles) in the exosuit swing into action. The actuators for an exosuit may be electric motors, or pneumatic or hydraulic devices. They boost the wearer's movement by amplifying, or increasing, their muscle power. In this way, a small, weak arm movement becomes a large, powerful arm movement.

Back injuries are common for workers who deal with heavy loads. One day, exosuits could wipe out workplace injuries.

Uses for Exosuits

Exosuits are increasingly being used to help people with muscle diseases and people who are partially paralyzed. Amazingly, leg exosuits can help people walk. Exosuits also have military and industrial uses. Some industrial exosuits boost arm and back power, while others transfer some of the weight of the lifted object onto the ground, through the legs of the exoskeleton.

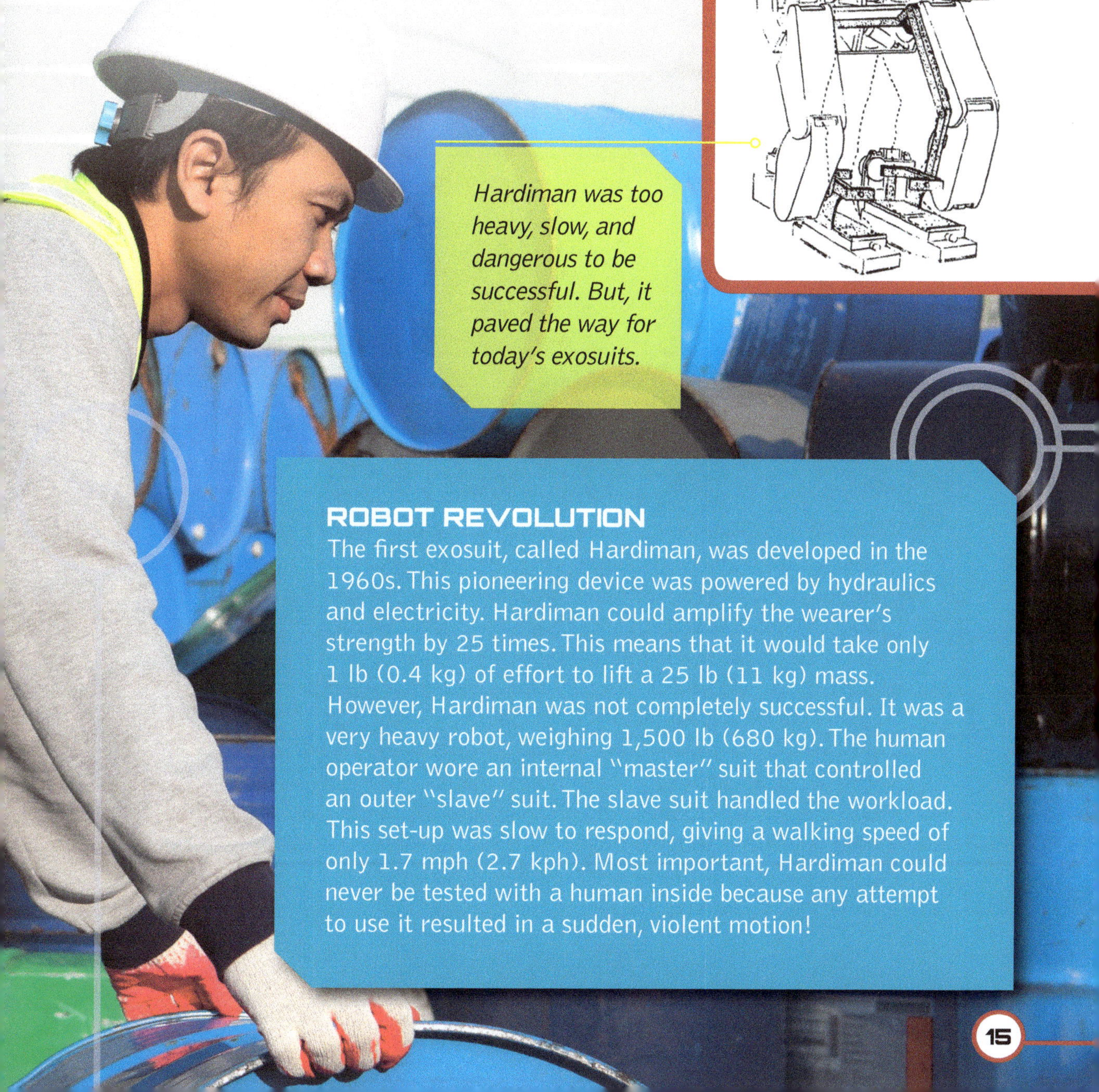

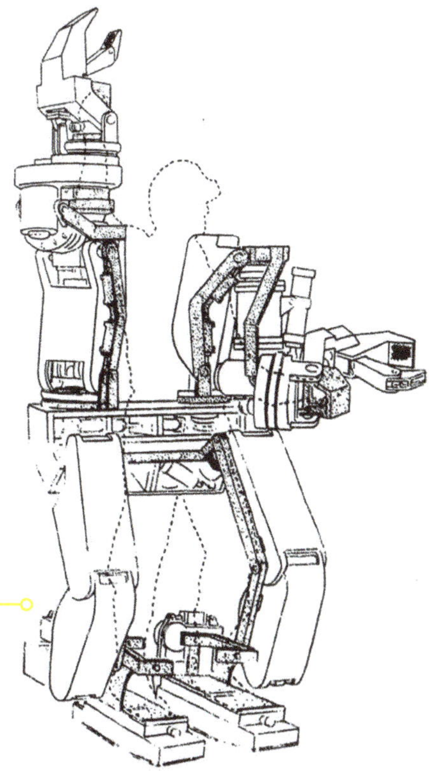

Hardiman was too heavy, slow, and dangerous to be successful. But, it paved the way for today's exosuits.

ROBOT REVOLUTION

The first exosuit, called Hardiman, was developed in the 1960s. This pioneering device was powered by hydraulics and electricity. Hardiman could amplify the wearer's strength by 25 times. This means that it would take only 1 lb (0.4 kg) of effort to lift a 25 lb (11 kg) mass. However, Hardiman was not completely successful. It was a very heavy robot, weighing 1,500 lb (680 kg). The human operator wore an internal "master" suit that controlled an outer "slave" suit. The slave suit handled the workload. This set-up was slow to respond, giving a walking speed of only 1.7 mph (2.7 kph). Most important, Hardiman could never be tested with a human inside because any attempt to use it resulted in a sudden, violent motion!

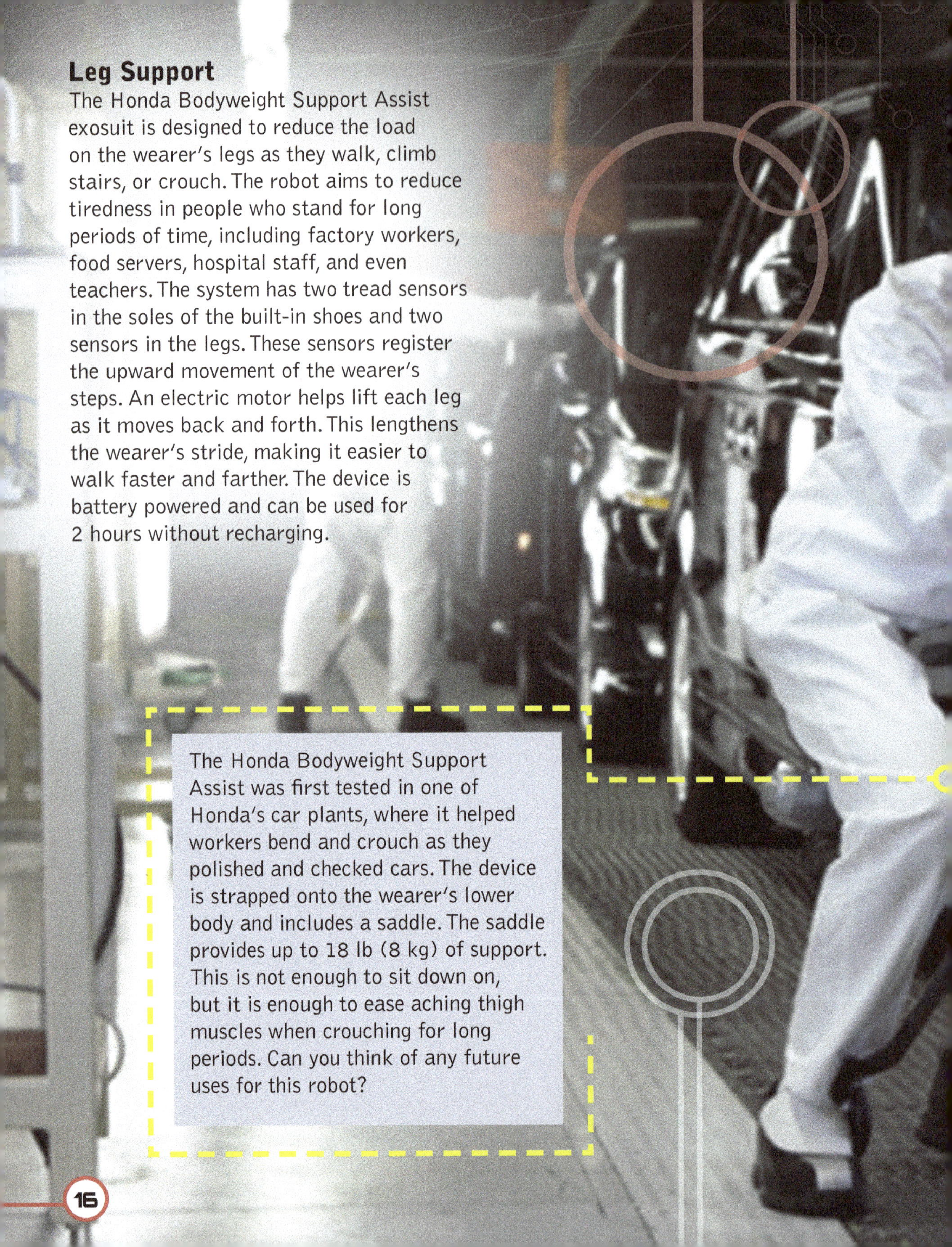

Leg Support

The Honda Bodyweight Support Assist exosuit is designed to reduce the load on the wearer's legs as they walk, climb stairs, or crouch. The robot aims to reduce tiredness in people who stand for long periods of time, including factory workers, food servers, hospital staff, and even teachers. The system has two tread sensors in the soles of the built-in shoes and two sensors in the legs. These sensors register the upward movement of the wearer's steps. An electric motor helps lift each leg as it moves back and forth. This lengthens the wearer's stride, making it easier to walk faster and farther. The device is battery powered and can be used for 2 hours without recharging.

The Honda Bodyweight Support Assist was first tested in one of Honda's car plants, where it helped workers bend and crouch as they polished and checked cars. The device is strapped onto the wearer's lower body and includes a saddle. The saddle provides up to 18 lb (8 kg) of support. This is not enough to sit down on, but it is enough to ease aching thigh muscles when crouching for long periods. Can you think of any future uses for this robot?

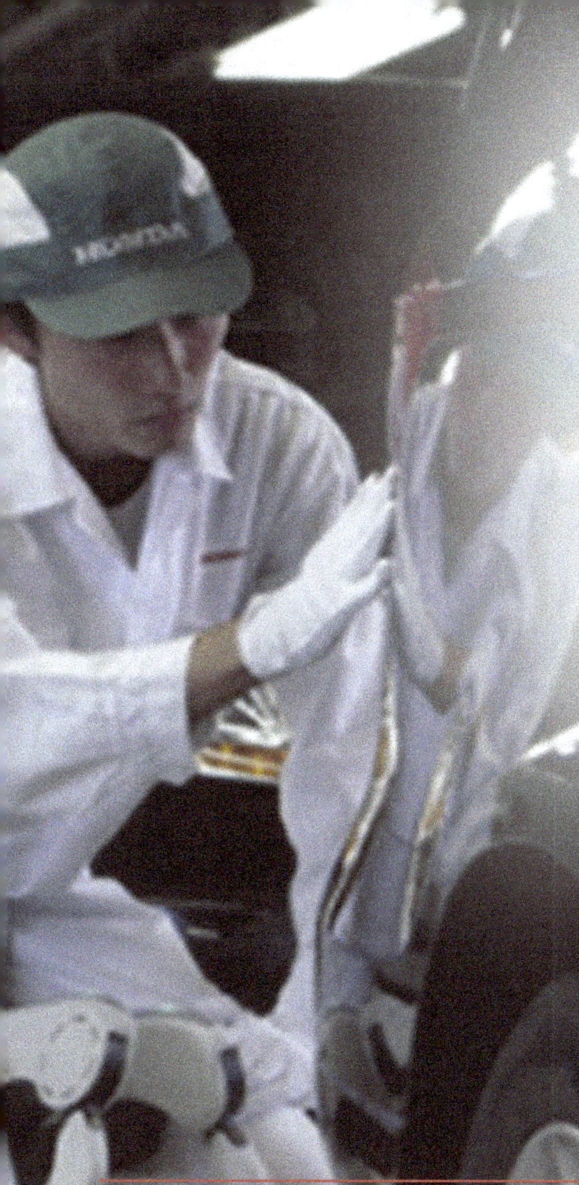

The device is based on research carried out with Honda's ASIMO, the "Advanced Step in Innovative Mobility" robot. ASIMO is a humanoid walking robot developed in 2000 and updated many times since. ASIMO has a walking speed of 1.7 mph (2.7 kph) and a running speed of 3.7 mph (6 kph). When any robot walks, it must find the "zero moment point" with every step. This moment is when the foot's contact with the ground does not produce any horizontal, or sideways, movement. In other words, the robot does not fall over as it transfers its weight from one foot to the other. Humans effortlessly find the zero moment point by tilting their bodies and moving their legs in perfect balance. Toddlers and robots have trouble finding the zero moment point.

ASIMO is one of the world's most advanced two-legged, walking robots. It can go up and down stairs and kick a ball. Its sensors tell it how hard and fast it is placing each foot on the floor. This is essential for keeping balance. ASIMO's breakthroughs helped produce Honda's exosuits.

HAL, which stands for "Hybrid Assistive Limb," is a range of robots that offer support for the legs, lower back, upper body, or whole body. Some elderly people and people with physical disabilities or injuries already use leg-support versions of HAL. Other versions of HAL are intended for heavy work in factories, hospitals, and construction, as well as rescue work after disasters, like earthquakes.

Work on HAL began in 1991, when a Japanese professor of robotics, Yoshiyuki Sankai, began to map out how nerve signals from the brain control movements. Next, Sankai had to figure out how to use sensors to detect those signals. He also developed a program that remembers the walking patterns, or gait, of the wearer the first time they use the exosuit. The robot is then able to keep fully in step with the wearer on future uses. Back in 1997, early versions of HAL weighed 49 lb (22 kg) and had to be wired to a computer. Today's full bodysuit weighs 22 lb (10 kg) and the battery and computer controller are strapped around the wearer.

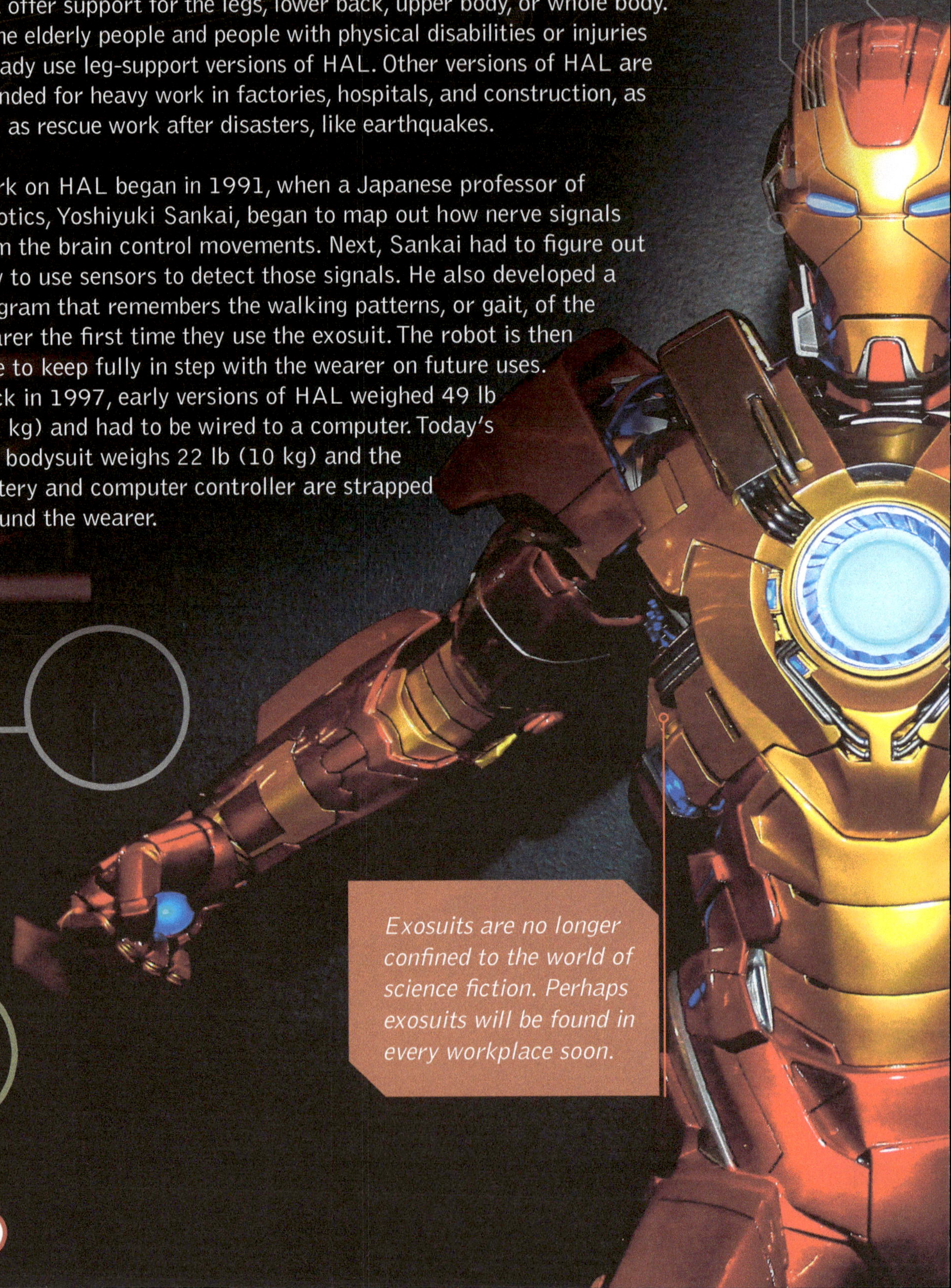

Exosuits are no longer confined to the world of science fiction. Perhaps exosuits will be found in every workplace soon.

HAL 5 is a full-body suit that strengthens the movements of the arms, legs, and body.

The back-support version of HAL is designed to help the user bend and lift heavy objects. It reduces strain on the muscles of the lower back and may cut down the number of work-related back injuries. It weighs only 6.4 lb (2.9 kg). To make HAL safe, it is programmed to help the wearer lift an object that they could lift alone. It simply reduces the effort needed to do so. It does not allow the wearer to lift objects that are way beyond their own ability. The level of assistance can be increased and decreased by easy-to-use buttons.

ROBOT REVOLUTION

If you are a fan of science fiction or comic-book characters like Iron Man, you will be familiar with many of the functions that an exosuit could perform. Iron Man's exosuit is armored, is capable of flight, and has built-in weapons and sensors. Some exosuits currently in development sound like they are inspired by Iron Man. The pioneering Springtail Exoskeleton Flying Vehicle is combined with a jet pack. It would allow the wearer to fly through the air at 70 mph (113 kph). The U.S. military is also working on exosuits that would include body armor and computerized fabrics that would monitor breathing and heart rates.

CHAPTER 3

ON THE MOVE

Mobile robots are those that are able to move around. Some travel only through their own workplace, while others can move through rugged and hilly landscapes. Although some robots may slide or roll to get about, most industrial robots move on wheels, tracks, or legs.

Fully autonomous mobile robots need a range of sensors and equipment to allow them to judge their position, navigate through their environment, and avoid collisions. Many mobile robots use the Global Positioning System (GPS) to know where they are. GPS is made possible by a network of about 30 satellites that orbit, or travel around, Earth. Each satellite broadcasts radio signals that give information about its position and the current time. These signals travel to a GPS receiver on Earth at the speed of light, 186,000 mps (300,000 kms). The GPS receiver picks up the signals and because it knows the position of the satellite, the time the signal left the satellite, and the speed it traveled, it can calculate the distance to each satellite. As long as at least three satellites are above the horizon at any given time, a GPS receiver can figure out where it is.

Early industrial mobile robots were based on the design of bomb disposal robots, like this one.

Distance

Robots use odometry to calculate how far they have traveled from their point of departure. In the simplest terms, if a robot's computer knows the circumference of its wheels (the distance around the outside of them), as well as how many times its wheels have rotated, it can figure out how far it has moved. Robots have Light Detection And Ranging (LIDAR) sensors to judge the distance of other objects and how fast they are approaching. This is essential for avoiding collisions. LIDAR uses ultraviolet (UV) light. The robot shines the UV light at an object and times how long the light takes to return to its source. It can then calculate the object's distance and speed.

A vacuum cleaning robot travels on wheels, avoiding furniture.

ROBOT REVOLUTION

Humans can judge distance and perceive 3D structures because they have two eyes. The eyes are located a short distance apart on the front of the head. The human brain receives two slightly different images of an object at the same time. The slight differences between the two images are processed in the brain to give what is called depth perception. Today's robot pioneers have stereovision cameras, which are used to get the same effect. The cameras record images from two slightly different locations. A computer program compares the two images to find the parts that match. The amount that any object has moved is called the disparity. This disparity is used to calculate distance and detect 3D objects.

The fastest robots have wheels—autonomous cars have reached 150 mph (240 kph). However, wheels are only efficient over even ground. In mines, on construction sites, on snow, or on marshy ground, wheeled robots would get stuck. To contend with uneven ground, high-mobility robots run on tracks. Tracks are continuous bands of ridged treads or plates. They are commonly seen on military tanks and construction vehicles. The larger the surface area of the tracks, the more the weight of the vehicle is spread out, which enables it to cross soft ground without sinking in. The ridges on the tracks prevent slippage.

Chaos

The Chaos high-mobility robot has four independently rotating tracks. Unlike the tracks on a tank, Chaos's tracks do not remain flat on the ground. Instead they flip, end over end. As a result, Chaos's style of movement is a little like swimming, using four paddling limbs. Chaos can use its track design to climb stairs or steep slippery slopes. Tracks are one of the slower means of robot motion. Chaos has a top speed of 6.5 mph (10.5 kph).

Chaos is a robotic platform, which means it is designed to be a load carrier. It can carry up to 100 lb (45 kg) without slowing down. Chaos's load might be goods or equipment, or it might be a robotic arm, camera, or other sensors. With these robotic attachments, Chaos can be used for tasks from the inspection of remote pipelines to carrying battlefield supplies. Can you think of advantages and disadvantages to using robots on a battlefield?

This four-legged, horse-like robot was designed by the U.S. Department of Defense.

ROBOT REVOLUTION

Pioneering robot engineers have experimented with different designs for walking robots, taking their inspiration from the natural world. Many bipedal, or two-legged, robots walk and run in a similar way to humans, by bending at the knees. Currently, the fastest of these human-like runners is the Michigan Anthropomorphic Biped with Electronic Legs (Mabel), which can reach 6.8 mph (10.9 kph). Far faster is a bipedal robot called Raptor, whose running style mimics the dinosaur, *Velociraptor*. It has an outstretched tail for balance and has reached 28.58 mph (46 kph). Its legs are springy, extra-strong carbon blades, similar to those worn by human amputee sprinters. A little faster is Cheetah, a four-legged robot with a running style that mimics the big cat. Its top speed is 29 mph (47 kph), slightly faster than human sprinter Usain Bolt, whose top speed is 28 mph (45 kph).

Robots are on the rise in warehouses around the world. Warehouses are storage areas where products or materials are kept, usually ordered in a grid system. The location of each product or material can be carefully recorded using a coordinate system based on the letters x, y, and z. This system makes it easy to command a robot to move to a particular spot: move x rows across the warehouse, move y rows down the warehouse, then move up z shelves.

Mobile robots equipped with grabbers, sensors, and platforms for carrying can travel through a warehouse, picking products, moving them to a packing area, then loading the packaged product onto vans or a robotic delivery system. Some cutting-edge warehouse robots have sensors and flexible grippers that allow them to work with products that are askew on a shelf, or stacked in a variety of different ways.

Eve

Eve is a robot designed specially for warehouse and factory work. This robot can carry large products or materials weighing up to 1 ton (0.9 mt), roughly the weight of a polar bear. Eve is intended to take over from human-driven delivery systems, like forklift trucks and "tugger trains." A tugger train is a train-like system used to carry materials through a workplace, either pulled along by hand or driven by an engine.

Eve rolls smoothly along, delivering materials to wherever they are needed.

The use of robots for this work means that human workers no longer have to do any heavy and dangerous lifting. Eve's program instructs the robot not only to navigate from place to place independently but also to calculate and choose the quickest route. Most important, Eve's sensors warn when a collision is likely to take place, making the robot safe to use around humans.

Eve is designed for logistics. Logistics is the process of transporting goods to customers. The process starts when a company receives a customer's order. The information is sent to a warehouse. The product is picked and packaged, then sent out for delivery. Large online stores are leading the way in using robots for logistics. These stores already use many warehouse robots and may, in the near future, cut humans out of the process even further by using drones for delivery to customers. The benefits of using robots for logistics are increased safety, speed, and accuracy, and lowered cost. Robots can pick, package, and deliver products all through the night and on holidays. Can you think of any drawbacks to using a robotic workforce for logistics? Give reasons for your answer.

Driverless Vehicles

The first on-the-road trials of a fully autonomous electric bus took place in Perth, Australia, in 2016. The robotic bus is called Intellibus and it can carry up to 11 passengers. There are five levels of vehicle automation. At level 0, the human driver is in complete control of the vehicle. At level 1, the vehicle has an automated function, like cruise control, which can be turned on briefly while driving. Cruise control maintains the vehicle's speed without the driver touching the accelerator or brake. At level 2, the vehicle has partial automation. For example, the cruise control could slow the vehicle to keep a safe distance from the vehicle ahead. At level 3, the driver can turn on full automation in simpler environments, like freeways. The vehicle can then accelerate, brake, and swerve to avoid obstacles on its own. At level 4, the vehicle drives itself in all but a few environments, such as severe weather. At level 5, the vehicle does everything automatically. The only human intervention necessary is to set the vehicle's destination before departure. The Intellibus has level 4 automation.

Automated vehicles need a range of sensors to detect pedestrians, other vehicles, traffic lights, and changes in road conditions. Sensors include stereovision cameras, to see other objects and judge their distance, and LIDAR sensors, to measure the speed at which other vehicles are approaching. When these sensors tell the vehicle's computer controller that a collision is about to happen, it applies the emergency brakes. To navigate its way through city streets, the Intellibus uses a GPS system similar to those in ordinary vehicles. It also uses odometry to estimate how far it has traveled from its starting point.

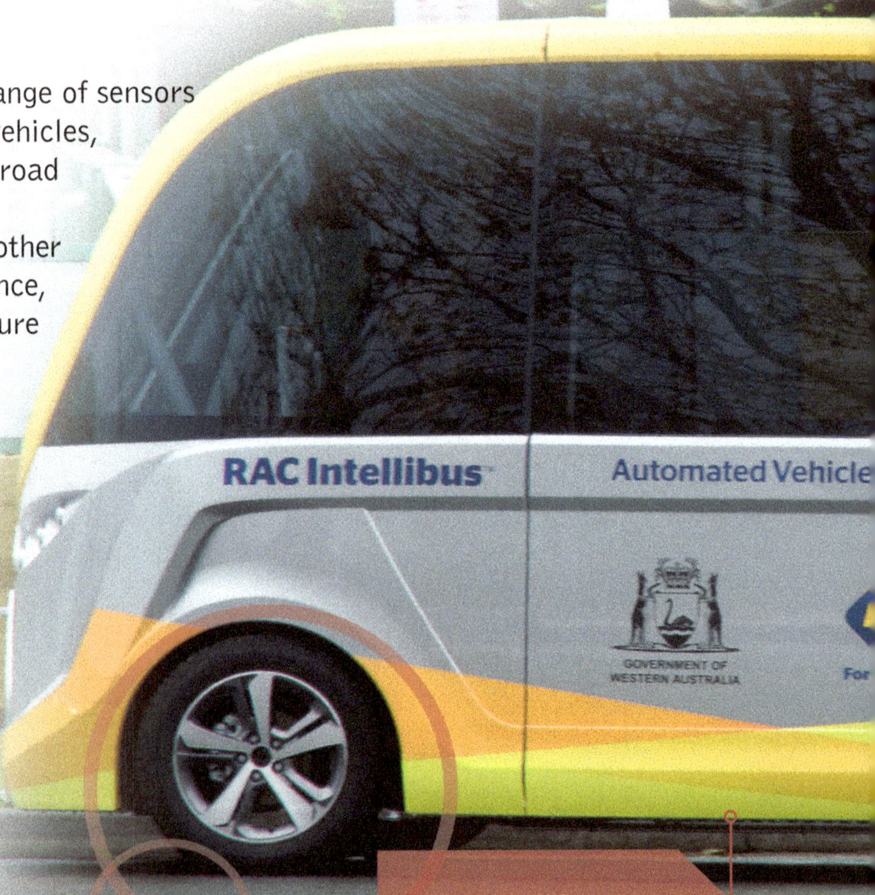

The Intellibus navigates its way through city streets.

A Google driverless car uses LIDAR.

ROBOT REVOLUTION

Driverless cars sound scary, but 90 percent of car crashes are caused by human error. In a fully autonomous car, there is no chance of human error. In a semiautonomous vehicle, the vehicle can correct the driver when they make a mistake. For example, the vehicle takes control if it is moving too fast for the road conditions or if it is veering out of the lane.

However, until the robotic technology is perfected, and until every car on every road is robotic, the possibilities for error still exist. Once every vehicle is driverless, each vehicle could communicate with every other vehicle. This could ease traffic jams, as vehicles would automatically know which intersections to avoid.

Huge semi-autonomous cranes lift containers from ships.

Autonomous trucks are used to transport heavy goods and materials in many industries, from mining to construction. At container ports, automated transportation is becoming more and more common. Every year, about 18 million containers packed with goods and materials make 200 million trips across the world's oceans on board container ships.

A standard container is 8 ft (2.4 m) wide, 8.5 ft (2.6 m) high, and either 20 ft (6 m) or 40 ft (12 m) long. The containers are unloaded from ships at a port and transferred to trucks or railroad cars for transport over land. Given their size and weight, the containers require immense cranes and trucks to move them. This heavy, dull, but extremely careful work is perfect for robots. The faster the robots can work, the more ships can dock in the port.

Altenwerder

The Container Terminal Altenwerder at the busy port of Hamburg, Germany, uses pioneering robots for most of its operations. It was one of the first ports to use an automated system. Cranes, which have automated functions but are overseen by a human worker using remote control, lift each container off its ship and onto an automated trolley. The container is slid onto a driverless truck. Each truck receives its destination from the port's central computer system, which communicates with its army of trucks using radio waves. The truck drives the container to the correct temporary storage area, where a robotic gantry (overhead rail system) carries the container to its resting place. Each container is stored in the right spot so that it can be easily reached when it is time to load it up again for onward travel. The whole process is monitored on a computer system from a central control room.

At Container Terminal Altenwerder, automated trucks find their way through the port using transponders in the road surface. Transponders are devices that send and receive messages. Each transponder constantly transmits its exact location. The trucks orient themselves in relation to the different transponders. The vehicles are also equipped with GPS. Odometry allows the trucks to know how far they have traveled by calculating how many times their wheels have turned. Human workers are not allowed within the automated area of the port, which is behind security fences. If someone does enter the area, the entire automated system shuts down. Do you think these safety precautions are sufficient?

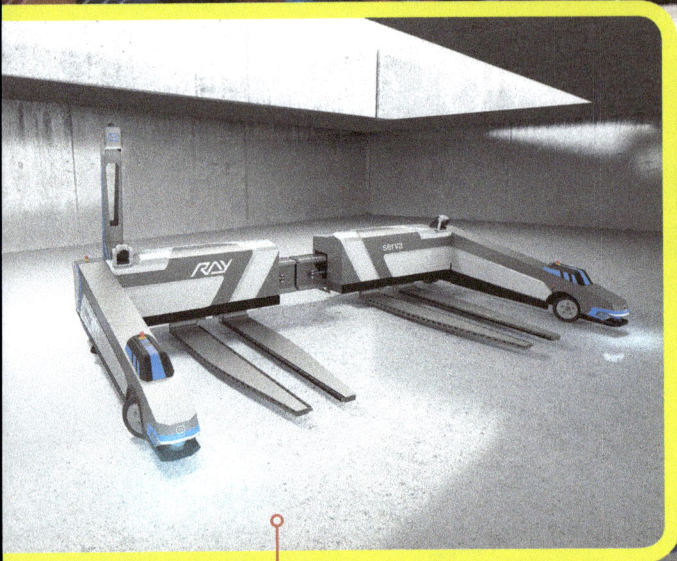

A benefit of the Ray parking system is that drivers do not need to squeeze their car into a tight space in a parking garage, where scrapes often happen.

Finding a parking spot can be a problem. As more and more cars are on our roads, this problem is set to get worse. A pioneering parking robot called Ray offers a solution. In 2014, Ray went into use at Düsseldorf Airport, Germany. A customer drives their own car into one of Ray's drop-off stations. They use a touchscreen computer to input their flight details, so Ray knows when they will be returning. The customer then walks away. Ray memorizes the car's license plate so the car can be found later. It also takes photos of the car from all angles, to prove it has not been damaged during parking. Ray then pulls alongside the car and slides four flat arms under its body—two arms go on either side of the front wheels, and the other two arms go around the back wheels. Each pair of arms slowly grips each pair of wheels. Ray lifts the car, glides along on its own wheels, and carries the car to a parking spot. Ray can carry cars weighing up to 3 tons (2.7 mt). A large passenger car weighs about 2 tons (1.8 mt).

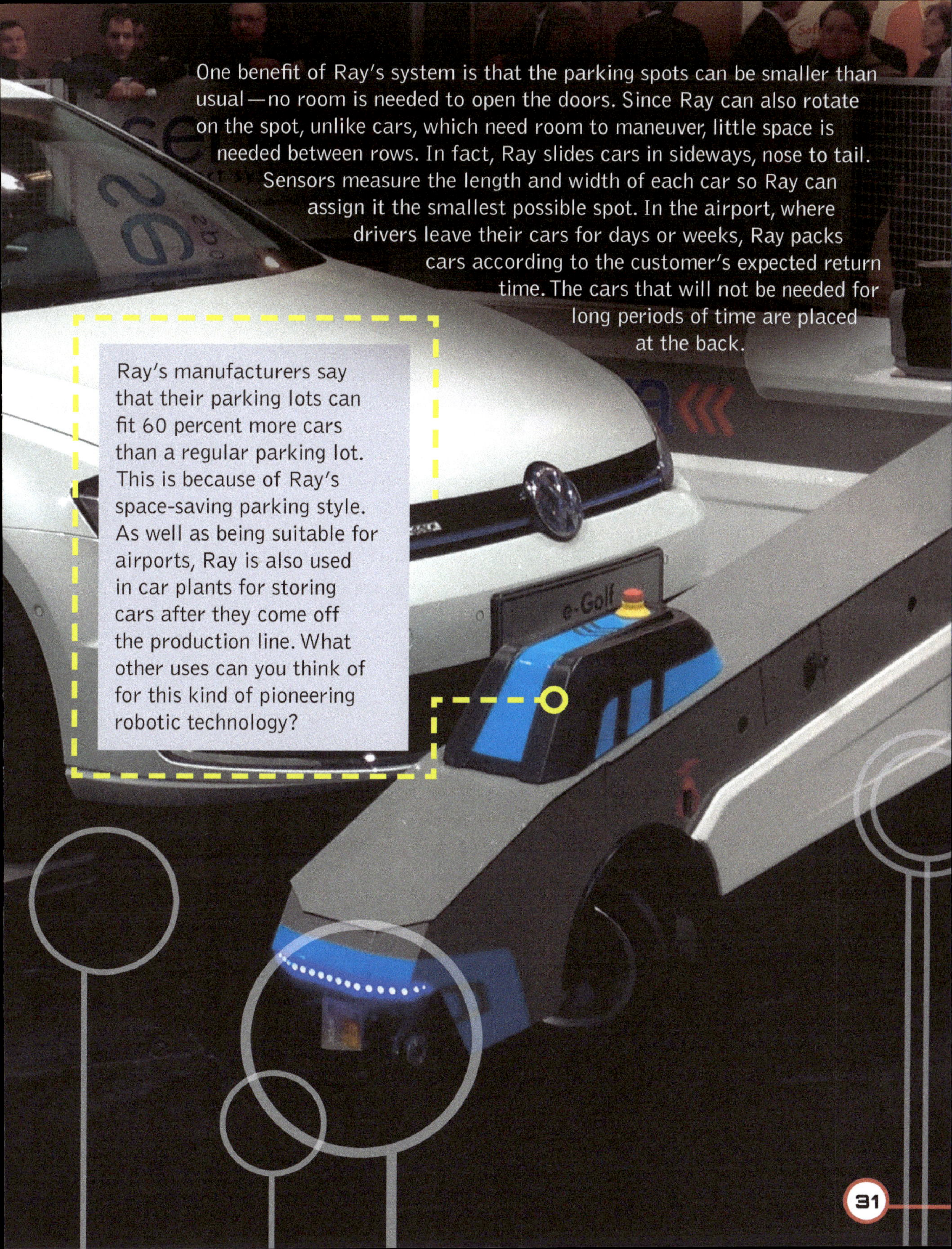

One benefit of Ray's system is that the parking spots can be smaller than usual—no room is needed to open the doors. Since Ray can also rotate on the spot, unlike cars, which need room to maneuver, little space is needed between rows. In fact, Ray slides cars in sideways, nose to tail. Sensors measure the length and width of each car so Ray can assign it the smallest possible spot. In the airport, where drivers leave their cars for days or weeks, Ray packs cars according to the customer's expected return time. The cars that will not be needed for long periods of time are placed at the back.

Ray's manufacturers say that their parking lots can fit 60 percent more cars than a regular parking lot. This is because of Ray's space-saving parking style. As well as being suitable for airports, Ray is also used in car plants for storing cars after they come off the production line. What other uses can you think of for this kind of pioneering robotic technology?

The average person produces about 1,300 lb (590 kg) of household waste every year. In some areas, household waste is taken to large public containers, from where it is collected by truck. In other areas, waste is collected door-to-door, with human garbage collectors loading it into a vehicle or wheeled cart. Some people want to use robots for this messy and time-consuming job.

DustCart

In Peccioli, Italy, the world's first garbage-collecting robot, called DustCart, does exactly that. Customers can order a collection by DustCart using their smartphone. The robot rolls on its six wheels to the customer's door, using GPS to navigate and laser sensors to avoid collisions. On arrival, DustCart sounds a siren to alert the customer.

A lot of thought has been devoted to the interaction between the human customer and the robot. DustCart has a moving head and eyes that light up, giving the robot an approachable and less "machine-like" appearance. The customer uses DustCart's touchscreen to open the container in its "body." When the customer drops their garbage inside, DustCart's "voice" thanks them through its speakers.

The way that we collect and handle garbage is a key issue around the world. This is an area where pioneering robots are starting to help.

DustCart has been popular in Peccioli. The challenge is now to roll out the system on a wider scale.

ROBOT REVOLUTION

Inventors have been working on talking machines since the eighteenth century. In 1937–38, Homer Dudley invented the Voice Operating Demonstrator, or "Voder." This pioneering machine was the first to successfully recreate the effects of the human vocal tract—the vocal cords, throat, and mouth—which is how we make sounds. Pressing different keys and pedals produced different sounds, like a hissing noise for "s" or a buzzing sound for vowels. It took months of training for an operator to create words.

In the 1950s and 1960s, the first computer-based voice synthesizers appeared. They sounded robotic and were often hard to understand. Modern speech synthesizers can store set words or phrases, as is the case with DustCart, or they may include a computerized model of the vocal tract and use it to create any speech from scratch. Today, it is still usually possible to tell computer-generated speech from human speech because of its intonation, the rise and fall of the voice. Engineers are at work on computerized models that will be sensitive enough even to give the impression that the robot or computer is "smiling" as it speaks!

CHAPTER 4

FARMING

Robots are used for a growing number of agricultural tasks, from caring for farm animals to planting and harvesting crops. Farming robots are often called agribots. Pioneering robots are also used in related industries like forestry and the growing of ornamental plants for gardens and parks.

Lettuce farmers plant more seeds than they actually need so that they can be sure enough plants take root. However, if too many plants are allowed to grow to full size, they overcrowd one another, blocking out sunlight. Pioneering robot, LettuceBot, offers a quick and easy solution. First, LettuceBot identifies every plant. The robot then decides which plants should be allowed to grow and which should be removed, based on the health of the plants. The robot can make 5,000 decisions per minute. A row of sprayers destroys unwanted plants with herbicide. LettuceBot's program ensures even spacing and evenly sized lettuces. What other benefits does LettuceBot offer a farmer? Can you think of any disadvantages to LettuceBot?

Agribots are not yet widely used in farming because, at present, they cost thousands of dollars per robot. This makes them too expensive for all but the largest businesses. As costs fall, agribots may transform farming. As in manufacturing industries, farming robots can speed up processes, cut costs, and reduce the need for human labor.

Seasonal Work

Many farming tasks require a lot of manpower and are seasonal. Fruit picking is a key example. When the time comes for harvest, hundreds of workers are needed to choose ripe fruit, cut or pluck it, and package it. This must be done before the fruit spoils. Most human fruit pickers are not needed on the farm for the rest of the year. Robot fruit pickers are increasingly common, with strawberry, grape, and berry-picking robots currently the most widespread. These robots have sensors to identify ripe fruit, and end effectors designed for the size and nature of the particular fruit, with gentle graspers and cutters.

Widespread use of pesticides can kill fish in neighboring ponds and lakes.

ROBOT REVOLUTION

One criticism of modern farming methods is the widespread use of chemicals. Herbicides, which kill weeds, and pesticides, which kill insect pests, are sprayed across whole fields. Potentially harmful chemicals enter waterways, where they can damage the natural balance of plants and animals. Agribots equipped with sensors and sprayer end effectors can solve this problem by targeting only infected plants or specific weeds. In addition, agribots can reduce water and land use by spacing plants according to mathematically determined patterns.

A tractor is a powerful motorized vehicle that pulls farm machinery and other vehicles. It has large wheels with deep treads, which spread its weight and keep it from getting bogged down in mud. Implements towed behind a tractor include plows, used for overturning the soil ready for planting, manure spreaders for fertilizing the soil, and seed drills, which sow seeds at equal distances and depths. These implements work automatically—some of them are even robotic—with little input from the farmer. If the tractor itself is driverless, then all the farmer must do is check on the quality of the work.

These driverless tractors are at work in a Texas vineyard.

Driverless Tractors

There are two types of driverless tractors—fully autonomous and semiautonomous. In a fully autonomous tractor, the farmer monitors the work at a computerized control station. Several tractors and fields can be monitored from one station. Most fully autonomous tractors navigate a field by bouncing lasers off transponders positioned around the field. The tractor's sensors measure the time taken for the laser beams to return, which allows the tractor to calculate distance. Knowing the distance from all transponders in the field gives it an accurate position. Some tractors also use GPS, in the same way as driverless cars. LIDAR sensors keep driverless tractors from bumping into unexpected obstacles.

Semiautonomous tractors are programmed to follow a lead, human-driven tractor. The two vehicles use vehicle-to-vehicle technology. This is a wireless connection between the tractors that allows them to share information. The lead tractor determines speed and direction, and transmits the information to the driverless tractor.

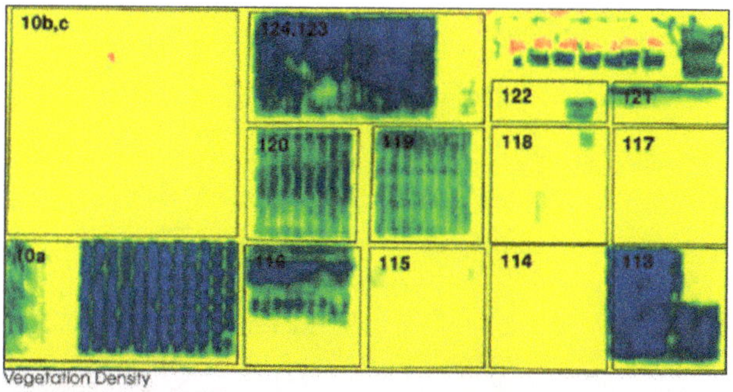

Vegetation Density

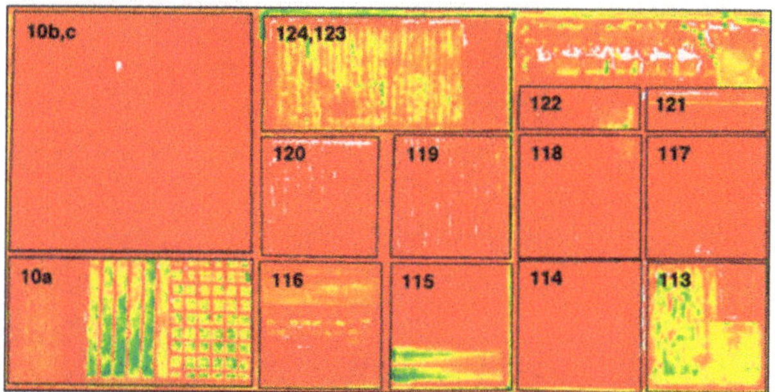

Water Deficit

Crop Stress

Precision farming uses images like these. The top image shows the quantity of plants (blue areas have most plants). The middle image shows dry soil (red). The bottom image shows stressed plants (red and yellow).

ROBOT REVOLUTION

A pioneering new farming method called precision agriculture uses driverless tractors as well as satellite, computer, and robotic technology. The aim is to get maximum crops from minimum land and resources. The farmer uses GPS and aerial photos taken by drones to carefully study the nature of the land and the quality of the soil. A computerized system combines this information with crop health information provided by robotic farm machinery or sensors mounted on ordinary farm machinery. The computer system can then inform the farmer exactly where more fertilizer, herbicide, or water is needed. In the future, the system will also be able to send out robotic fertilizers or weed-killers without involving the farmer at all.

There are 65,000 dairy farms in the United States. Some pioneering farms use robotic milkers.

In the United States, dairy cows produce about 185 billion lb (84 billion kg) of milk every year. It is sold in stores and is used to make dairy products like cheese and yogurt. Female cows produce milk after they have had a calf. The aim of a modern dairy farm is to produce as much milk as possible while keeping the cows healthy and comfortable. A key factor for a female cow's health is regular, gentle milking at least twice a day. Calves would naturally feed from their mother several times a day, so regular milking is the most natural method of dairy farming. In the past, dairy farms employed small armies of human milkers, but that is not the case today.

Milking Robots

The Astronaut milking robot consists of a milking stall, robotic arms, a milk-storage container, and a computer controller. Cows walk into the milking stall when they choose to be milked. All cows on a dairy farm are electronically tagged, so when a cow enters the stall, the robot's sensors identify it by its tag. If the cow has been milked too recently, an electronic gate allows it out of the stall. If it has not been milked recently, a robotic arm with a brush end effector cleans the cow's udders.

Next, the milking pumps attach gently to the cow's udders, positioning themselves with the help of a laser. The robot tests the quality of each cow's milk immediately. It checks the milk for signs of infection, as well as fat and protein content. If there is an abnormality, the milk is not added to the storage container, where it would spoil other milk, and the farmer is alerted.

The Astronaut robotic milker is teamed with a "Time for Cows" computerized management system. The system allows the farmer to review information on their phone or computer about each cow's milk quantity, quality, and health. Each cow is given a health score, based on these factors. The farmer can see right away if a cow is sick. A veterinarian can be called before any disease spreads to other cows, ultimately saving on veterinary costs. Healthy cows also produce more milk than stressed and unhealthy cows. Do you think that robotic milkers help dairy farms be profitable? Do you think they help farmers care for the wellbeing of their cows? Give reasons for your answers.

This team of HV-100s can reposition all these plants in just a couple of hours.

Robots and Plants

The HV-100 is a robot designed to work in plant nurseries and greenhouses. It is a mobile robot that is programmed to fetch and carry plant pots so that human workers do not have to do heavy lifting. An HV-100 can place 240 pots in one hour. It has sensors and flexible grippers that allow it to safely carry pots of a wide range of shapes and sizes.

When a crop of plants is being cultivated, the plant pots must be respaced as the plants grow, to allow each plant enough water and sunlight. Thousands of seasonal plants, like poinsettias, which are popular at Christmas, may need to be respaced within a few days. The HV-100's sensors and programming allow it to evenly space plant pots to allow enough room but also to reduce the waste of water, herbicide, and pesticide that is sprayed over them.

With safety sensors to prevent collisions, HV-100s work safely alongside people. They have a tough waterproof outer shell that is unaffected by rain, water sprinklers, dirt, and dust. This means that they can work in all weather conditions and temperatures. Their wheels run smoothly on gravel, soil, and concrete. The robot's developers intend that future pioneering generations of HV-100 will also photograph and test plants as they are placed. A team of HV-100s could be linked to a computer control system that would allow the nursery owner to make judgments about the health and water requirements of its plants.

The HV-100 is designed to reduce the need for a large human workforce in nurseries and greenhouses. The work carried out by HV-100s—repeatedly bending and picking up heavy plants in hot weather—is exhausting for humans and can cause back injuries. Many industrial robots are aimed at reducing the need for this kind of human manual labor. Do you think that this is a benefit to employers? Do you think it is a benefit to workers? Give reasons for your answers.

Today's pioneering farming robots use cameras to recognize weeds. The robots' software analyzes the images of a plant and, using an algorithm, or a set of rules, identifies whether or not the plant is a weed. The algorithm is based on the differences between the leaves of common weeds and the leaves of the crop in question. The system is "taught" to recognize weeds. This is done by providing it with many images of weeds and other plants. The system must match up similarities and detect differences. Some agribots even have artificial intelligence. Over time, they are better able to tell the difference between crops and weeds that have very similar leaves. When an agribot detects a weed, it sprays on a drop of herbicide. It does not need to spray entire fields with herbicides, which could damage the environment. Agribots like this are now fairly common in flat fields where crops grow in orderly rows.

IBEX2 Robot

The IBEX2 is a weed-detecting agribot, but is able to work on far more difficult terrain, or ground. It runs on tracks based on those used by military and bomb disposal robots. The tracks allow it to work on hilly land, where sheep and cows often graze. In such areas, up to 10 percent of the land can be taken over by weeds that are not edible for herds. This kind of rough terrain is hard to manage with an ordinary vehicle, and impossible for most robots.

The IBEX2 is able to travel over mud and up slopes of up to 45 degrees. The IBEX2 navigates using GPS, helped by other data from maps and satellite photos. The weeds are targeted using a robotic arm with a spray end effector. Can you think of any disadvantages to using a robot like this?

This tractor is spraying an entire field with pesticides. Object-recognition programs will make widespread spraying a thing of the past.

ROBOT REVOLUTION

Many cutting-edge robots are programmed with object-recognition algorithms. These allow the robot to recognize a weed as a weed, or a human face as a human face. Your brain constantly uses image-recognition algorithms. You instantly recognize a dog as a dog, even though its breed might be different from other breeds you have seen. Your brain notices key points of similarity, even while it is aware of the differences. For a computer algorithm to work well it must be "taught" how to see similarities by being fed countless images of the particular objects. Today's best algorithms allow robots to identify the programmed objects despite differences in angle of view. Algorithms of this type can be applied to many areas of agriculture, like picking fruit that is ripe, or identifying common agricultural pests, such as aphids.

CHAPTER 5

IN THE AIR

An unmanned aerial vehicle (UAV), also called a drone, is an aircraft without a human pilot on board. Drones carry out flights that are too dangerous, repetitive, or awkward for humans. Industrial uses for drones include inspections and deliveries.

Drones were first developed as military machines in the twentieth century. However, there are now far more industrial drones in the air than military drones. By 2020, it is predicted there will be 2.7 million industrial drones over the United States alone. Most industrial drones are small and lightweight and can be launched by hand. To be lightweight, they need to have small batteries. This means that they run out of power quite rapidly. Light electric motors usually turn the battery's electrical energy into motion.

Autonomy

To be considered a drone, a UAV must have some degree of autonomy, or autopilot, provided by its onboard flight controller. In contrast, aircraft that are fully operated by remote control are not drones. Basic drones can hover in an exact position without human interference. The most sophisticated drones take off and land alone, avoid collisions, and plot their own route.

All drones have two parts: the aircraft itself and the ground-based control and monitoring system, which is operated by a human. Communication between the drone and the ground-based system is usually through radio waves. In order to fly autonomously, drones must be armed with a range of sensors and other technology. One standard piece of technology is a GPS chip that sends its location back to the ground controller. It also records the drone's takeoff location so it can return automatically. Another common sensor is a gyroscope. This is a ball or disk that is free to tilt and turn within its mount as it changes angle. Gyroscopes tell the drone if it is tilting, losing height, or being blown off course.

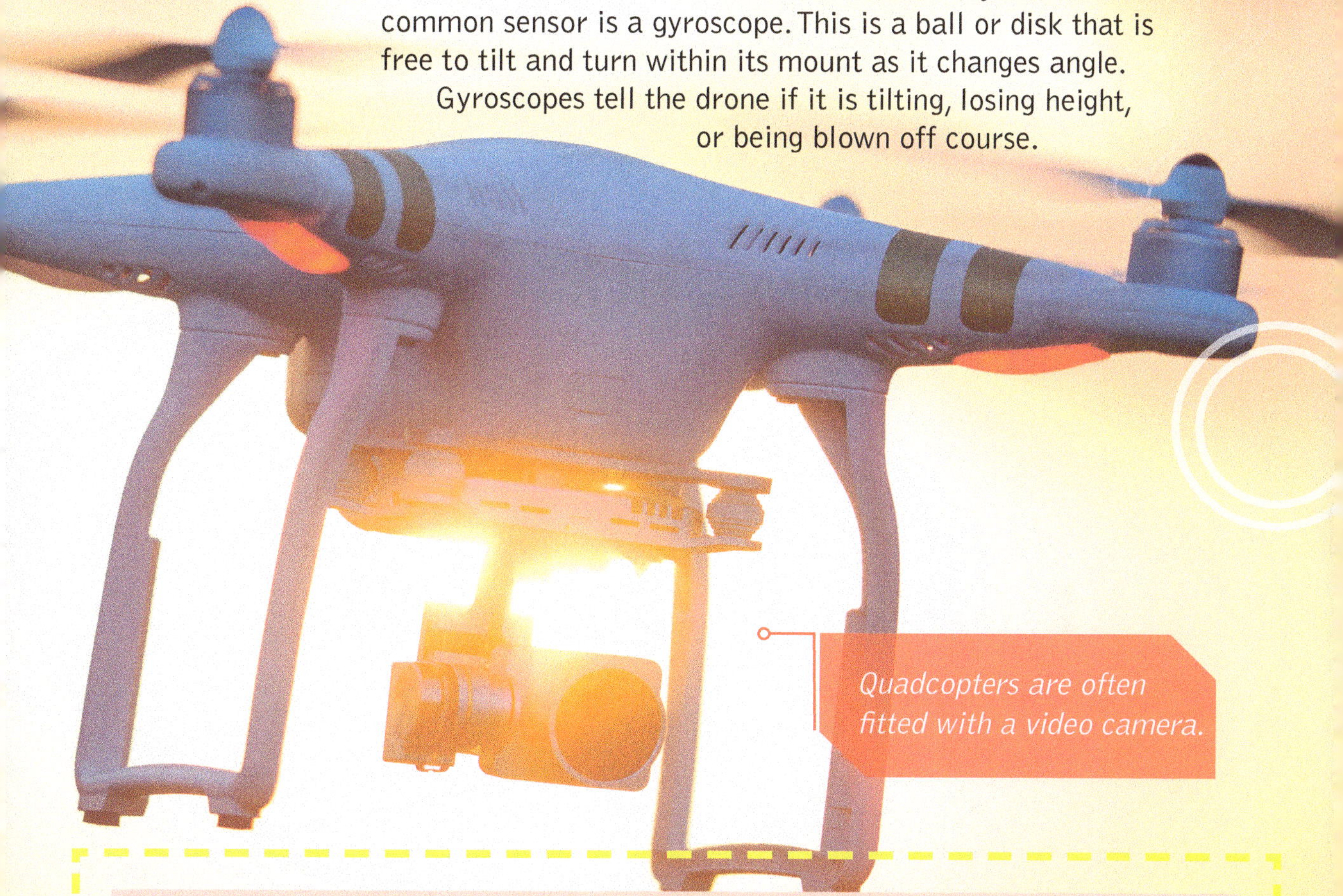

Quadcopters are often fitted with a video camera.

Many industrial drones are quadcopters. These are propelled by four rotors, or turning blades. Two blades turn clockwise and two turn counterclockwise. The aircraft changes direction and height by altering the speed of each rotor. Small quadcopters are easy to maneuver. The blades can also be fitted with guards to prevent injury. The quadcopter design is less suitable for larger, heavier aircraft because the larger the blades, the longer it takes to change their speed. Why are quadcopters particularly suitable for small drones? Give reasons for your answers.

Delivery drones can transport packages to customers, medical supplies to remote clinics, and materials from one part of a factory to another. Currently, most drone delivery services are at the testing phase. In the future, they are likely to transform the way we shop and communicate. Concerns about public safety, both for people on the ground and passenger aircraft, have stopped delivery services from getting government approval in most countries. Another key concern about drone deliveries is privacy, as drones can fly past windows and over backyards.

Parcelcopter

One of the first successful drone delivery trials took place in Germany, in 2016. DHL, the world's largest delivery company, used a "parcelcopter" to carry packages in a mountainous region of Bavaria for three months. In this snowy, windswept region, deliveries that would have taken 30 minutes by road were accomplished in just 10 minutes. The drones were able to independently load up in a special depot, and unload safely when they reached their destination.

A delivery drone, such as the DHL Paketkopter 2.0, needs a battery large enough to power its flight for a round trip. Since drones usually have a flight time of only 45 minutes, delivery drone networks will require many depots. Delivery drones will also need to have secure grippers. They must be capable of flying safely while holding heavy packages, or packages will need to be lightweight. Would you feel safe if delivery drones were flying over your head regularly?

ROBOT REVOLUTION

Micro drones are about the size of your hand, while the tiniest, called nano drones, fit in your palm. These tiny pioneering robots can be carried in a pocket. In the future, it will be possible to fold away their rotors to make them even more portable. Nano drones weigh around 1 oz (16 g), including batteries. Currently, their tiny batteries only offer nano drones a flying time of about 20 minutes, but soon it will be possible to buy the drones in packs of two along with a fast-working battery recharger. A possible industrial use would be taking a quick snapshot of the roof of a building or power line for inspection purposes.

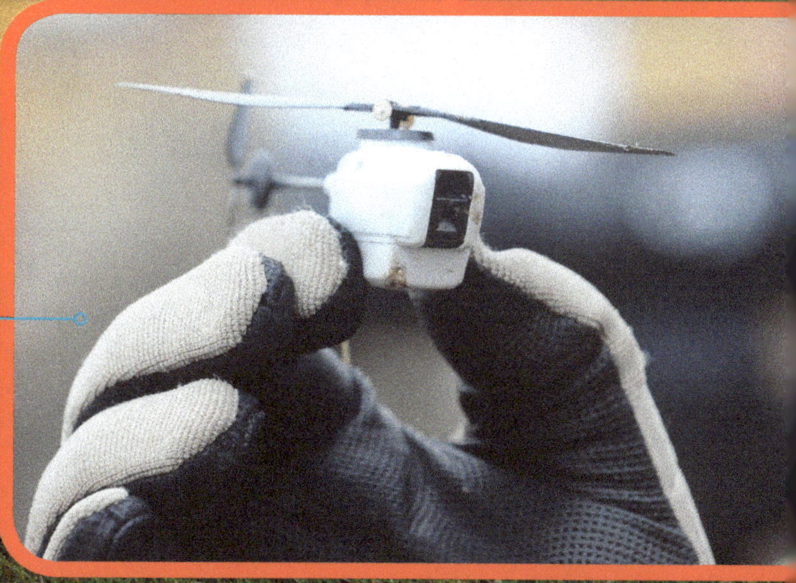

The Black Hornet nano drone is equipped with a camera.

Many larger drones have designs similar to manned aircraft. Some drones are in the form of conventional helicopters, with a single main rotor and a smaller tail rotor that prevents the helicopter from swinging around and around under the force of its main blade. Helicopter UAVs are usually larger and more powerful than quadcopters, so are able to carry greater loads. This makes them suitable for heavy-lifting tasks, particularly in conditions unsuitable or too dangerous for human pilots.

RMAX Drones

Japanese farmers have used Yamaha RMAX helicopter drones to spray their crops with pesticides or herbicides for the last 25 years. Most Japanese farms are quite small in size, and drones allow precise spraying at a lower cost than manned aircraft. Japan was the site of another important industrial use for these helicopter drones. In 2011, after the Tohoku earthquake damaged the Japanese Fukushima nuclear power plant, RMAXs were sent to monitor levels of radiation around the site. It was unsafe for humans to carry out this work.

A future use for this style of drones is likely to be in the delivery of goods and materials too heavy for small quadcopters. Perhaps they might even be used as driverless taxis. The first flights on single-passenger helicopter drones were announced by the city of Dubai, United Arab Emirates, in 2016.

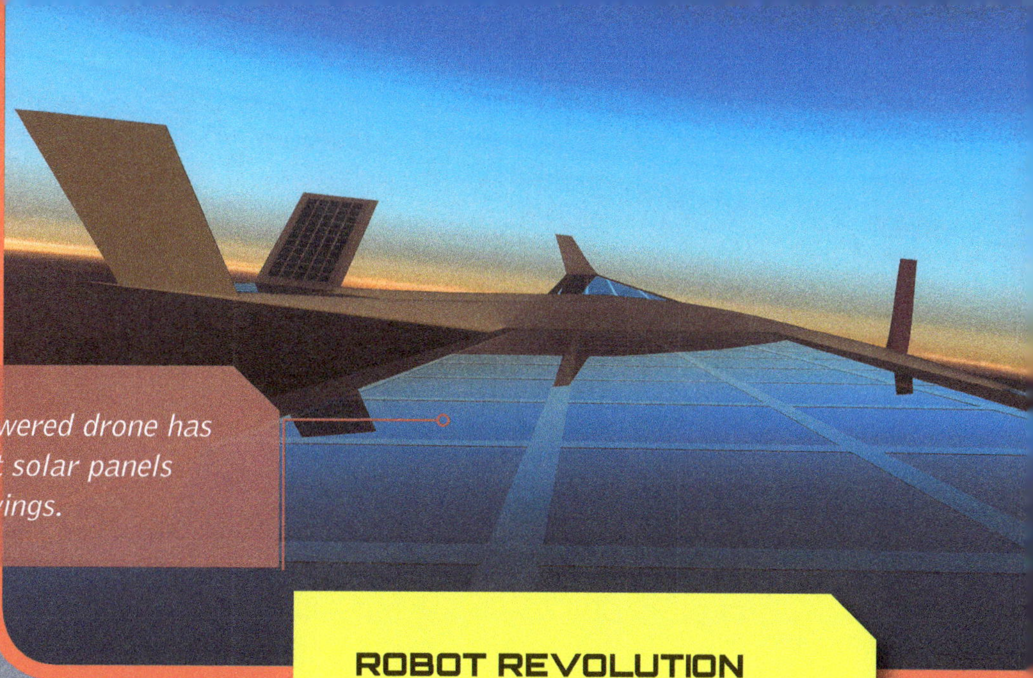

A solar-powered drone has lightweight solar panels along its wings.

This RMAX drone is being used to spray crops.

ROBOT REVOLUTION

A key issue for drone technology is that drone batteries usually need to be small, resulting in short flight times. The use of solar power may provide a solution. Drones could be fitted with solar cells, which turn the sun's energy into electricity. One drone already using this technology is the pioneering Solara 50, which is still in development. It is a fixed-wing aircraft, with horizontal wings to keep it airborne. Its solar cells will also charge batteries in its 165 ft (50 m) wide wings, allowing it to continue flying at night. It is planned that the drone will stay in the air for five years at a time, at a height of 65,000 ft (19,000 m). A fleet of Solara 50s is intended to hover over rural regions of Africa, offering free wireless connection to the internet via its radio transmitters.

Drones can take aerial videos and photos, to give a bird's-eye view of the ground or to inspect inaccessible objects and locations without the use of ladders, cranes, or manned airplanes. As well as being cheaper to fly than manned aircraft, small drones do little or no damage to the environment, even if they land in a delicate ecosystem. One exciting use for this kind of drone technology is in the television and film industries. The first Bond movie to use aerial footage shot by drones was *Skyfall*, in 2012. A Flying-Cam drone shot the opening sequence in which James Bond chases a terrorist across the rooftops of Istanbul on a motorbike.

Another key industrial use for drones is in the inspection of power lines, railroad tracks, gas pipelines, construction sites, and real estate. To protect their premises, businesses can use drones to carry out patrols instead of human security guards. Drones can also be used to monitor traffic flow and keep public transportation and logistics networks on the move.

This MD4-200 drone is going to inspect power lines using a visible light camera and thermal-imaging technology. Thermal imaging cameras show hot spots in the power lines, which are a sign of damage. In total, the drone can carry 9 oz (250 g) of sensors and cameras. It can fly at 18 mph (29 kph) for up to 30 minutes. It has a lightweight carbon-fiber body that withstands extremes of temperature and heavy rain. Using an ordinary tablet or personal computer, the human controller can set up the flight path in advance and analyze the data sent back by the drone. Can you think of any other uses for this kind of drone technology?

Drones and Maps

Mapping, using cameras, GPS, and laser sensors, is a common use for today's drones. These sensors enable the creation of topographical maps, which show the above ground features of the land. Drones can also be mounted with an array of special sensors that allow for geophysical mapping. This type of mapping shows below ground features. Sensors like infrared, magnetic (which detects metals and minerals), and ground-penetrating radar (which detects structures and materials) can build up a picture of the soil, rocks, and their resources. This is useful for industries like mining, as well as construction and archaeology.

An MD4-200 can withstand the high temperatures around fires and other hazards.

CHAPTER 6

HUMANOIDS

A humanoid robot has a shape that resembles the human body, with a head, arms, body, and sometimes legs. Some humanoid robots are programmed to copy human behavior, too. Humanoids are used for industrial tasks where looking or behaving like a human is beneficial.

The earliest industrial robots were nothing more than equipment. They performed simple tasks, as machines had done since the first modern-style factories appeared in the eighteenth century. The next generation of industrial robots had sensors to make them safer and to give their human users more information and control. The latest generation of industrial robots are intended to do far more than that. They are no longer pieces of equipment—they are partners for humans, working side-by-side with them, and sometimes taking over for humans entirely.

The pioneering Motoman humanoid robot, shown here building with LEGOs, is designed for use on factory lines.

If a robot is designed to work deep inside a factory and will have no interaction with human workers, there is no reason to make it humanoid. Its shape and behavior will be whatever is best suited to its task. However, where a robot works alongside humans, features that make the robot appear less "machine-like" and more "human" are a benefit.

Interaction with Humans

Today's industrial robots are taking on roles that would never have been considered for robots in the past. They interact with customers in industries from hospitality to banking. These new robot jobs are possible because of developments in the movement, speech, and behavior of robots, making them seem more "human" and friendlier than ever before. At present, human–robot interaction is still a novelty, which makes it fun and often funny. However, as the technology progresses, the interaction may become so streamlined that the human will forget they are talking to a robot.

Humans constantly adjust their behavior in response to their companions.

ROBOT REVOLUTION

Human behavior is complicated. Humans continue to learn how to behave and adapt to social situations throughout their lives. Humans also continuously change their behavior in response to others around them. Groundbreaking artificial intelligence programs try to copy the way that humans respond to each other—this is called social intelligence. As well as using sensors to detect human emotions, pioneering robots with social intelligence need to apply complex programs that simulate the way humans make decisions. To appear truly human, robots also need to simulate empathy, giving appropriate responses to human emotions. Experts in the study of the brain, psychology, and computer science are all involved in the development of social intelligence programs.

Most robotic arms, and other industrial robots, perform their specified task very quickly. They have heavy moving parts. Many of them continue with their task whether or not they have dropped a tool or a human has come dangerously close. This makes them unsafe for working side-by-side with humans. Sometimes, robotic parts of a production line are in separate areas of a factory from human workers, while at other times industrial robots are put in safety cages. However, some pioneering industrial robots are safe not just to work alongside humans but are designed to interact with them in a friendly way.

Baxter

Baxter is a robot with two arms, fixed to a pedestal on wheels. Baxter's computer can be programmed to make the arms carry out simple industrial tasks, like loading, moving, or placing materials. Essentially, Baxter is a pair of robotic arms, but one of the things that makes Baxter different is its "face," which is animated on a screen. Baxter has a range of facial expressions, showing concentration, sadness, a thought bubble when it needs assistance, and confusion when something goes wrong. These "emotions" are intended to make human coworkers feel friendly toward Baxter. Baxter also has distance sensors and cameras in its hands and arms that allow it to sense when it is about to knock into someone. The robot quickly reduces the force of its movements to prevent injury.

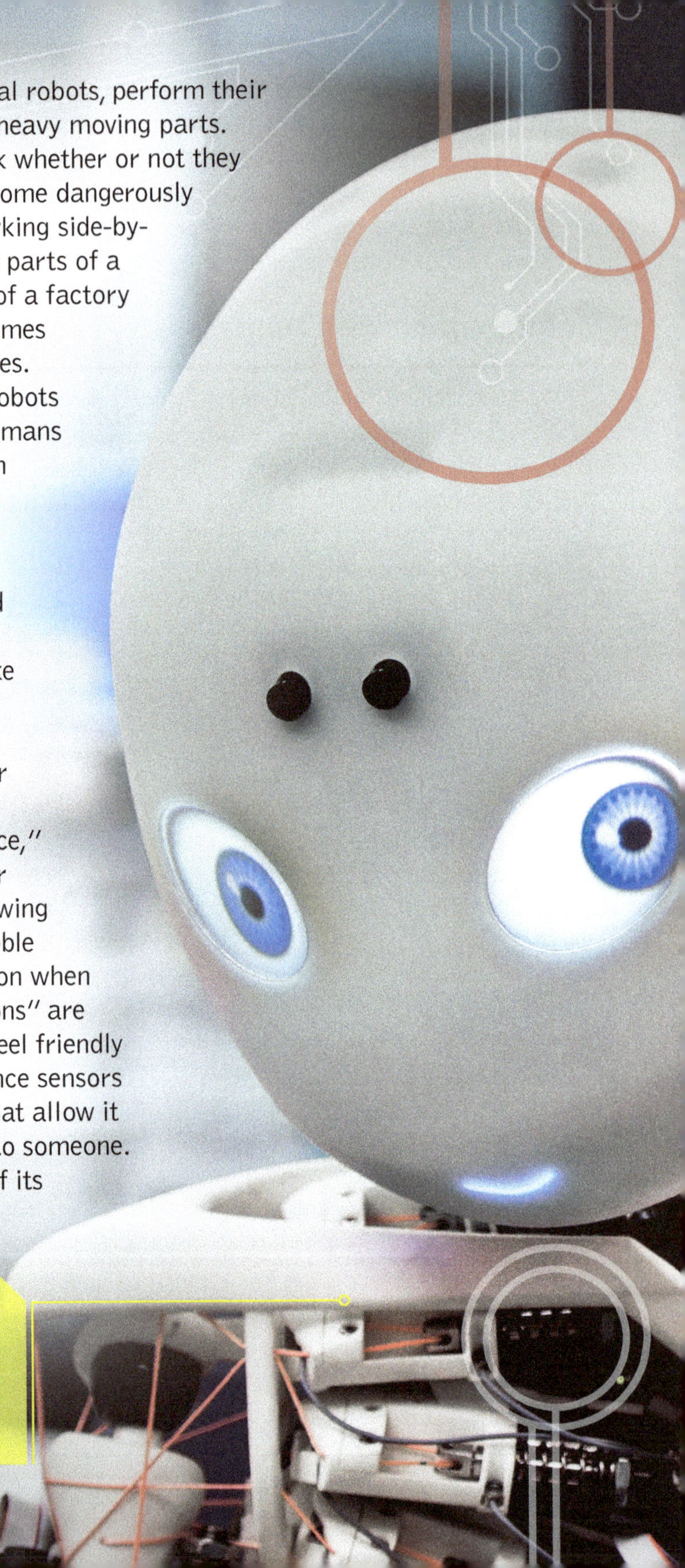

A humanoid's face is key to how it interacts with humans. Roboy has a particularly "sweet" face.

Baxter is designed to carry out repetitive tasks on a production line, working side-by-side with humans. As well as being safe and "friendly" toward human coworkers, Baxter must also be trained by a human. Unlike most robots, which are programmed by engineers using computer code, Baxter is trained to do jobs in a similar way to a human. A human coworker or supervisor must show Baxter how to do work by moving its arms in the required way. Baxter remembers and then repeats the motions. Do you think this feature would make Baxter more popular with human coworkers? Would you like to work alongside Baxter? Give reasons for your answers.

Nextage is a mobile industrial robot. It has human-like arms, a "head," and a body. It is able to carry out a range of production line tasks. The cameras on its end effectors take photographs from a range of different angles. This allows the robot's computer controller to build up a detailed picture of the 3D nature of the materials it is working with. Teamed with stereovision cameras on its "head," these cameras make Nextage's work very precise. Nextage's head can also turn to each side to adjust its field of vision. Since it is mounted on wheels, Nextage can move from workstation to workstation, increasing flexibility.

Programming

Most industrial robotic arms need a specialist to program them before they can be operated. In contrast, Nextage's coworkers or supervisor can tell it what tasks to perform and how to do them using a simple graphical user interface (GUI).

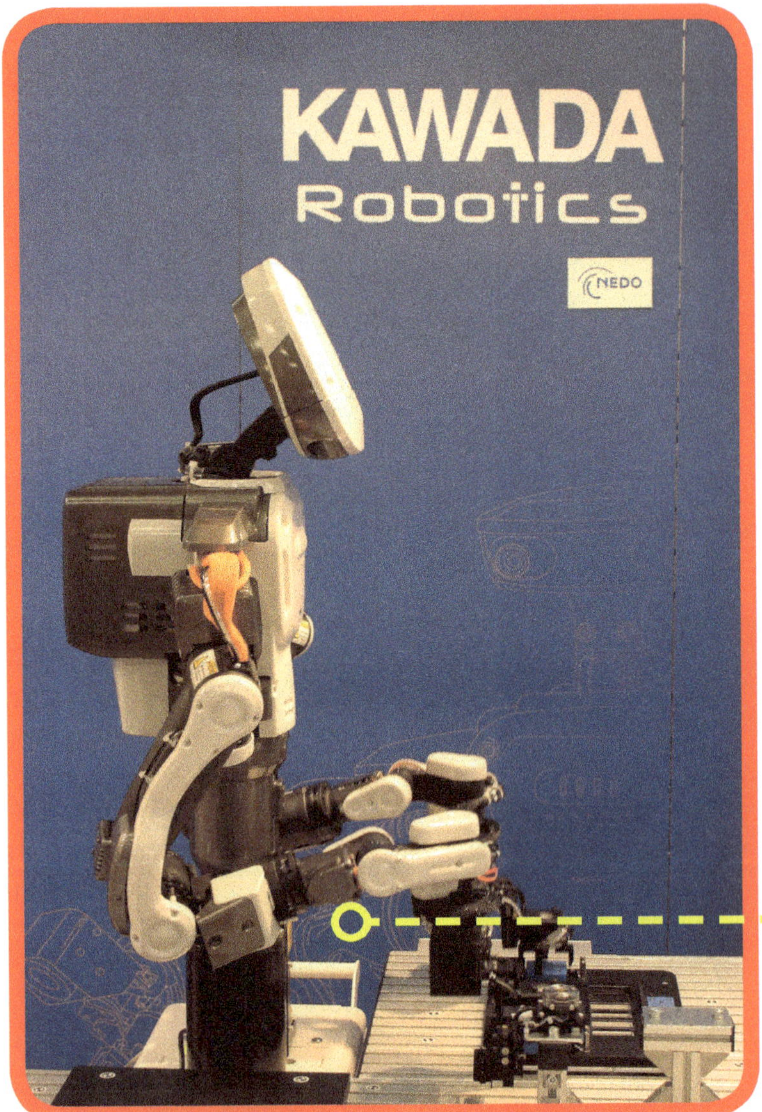

You use a GUI every time you use a smartphone or home computer. A GUI is all the drop-down menus and icons (pictures) that you click on to tell your computer what to do next. Today, we are so used to seeing GUIs that we hardly notice their existence. GUIs are very easy to use because many of the functions are shown in pictures instead of words. They are designed to be easy to understand, even from a young age.

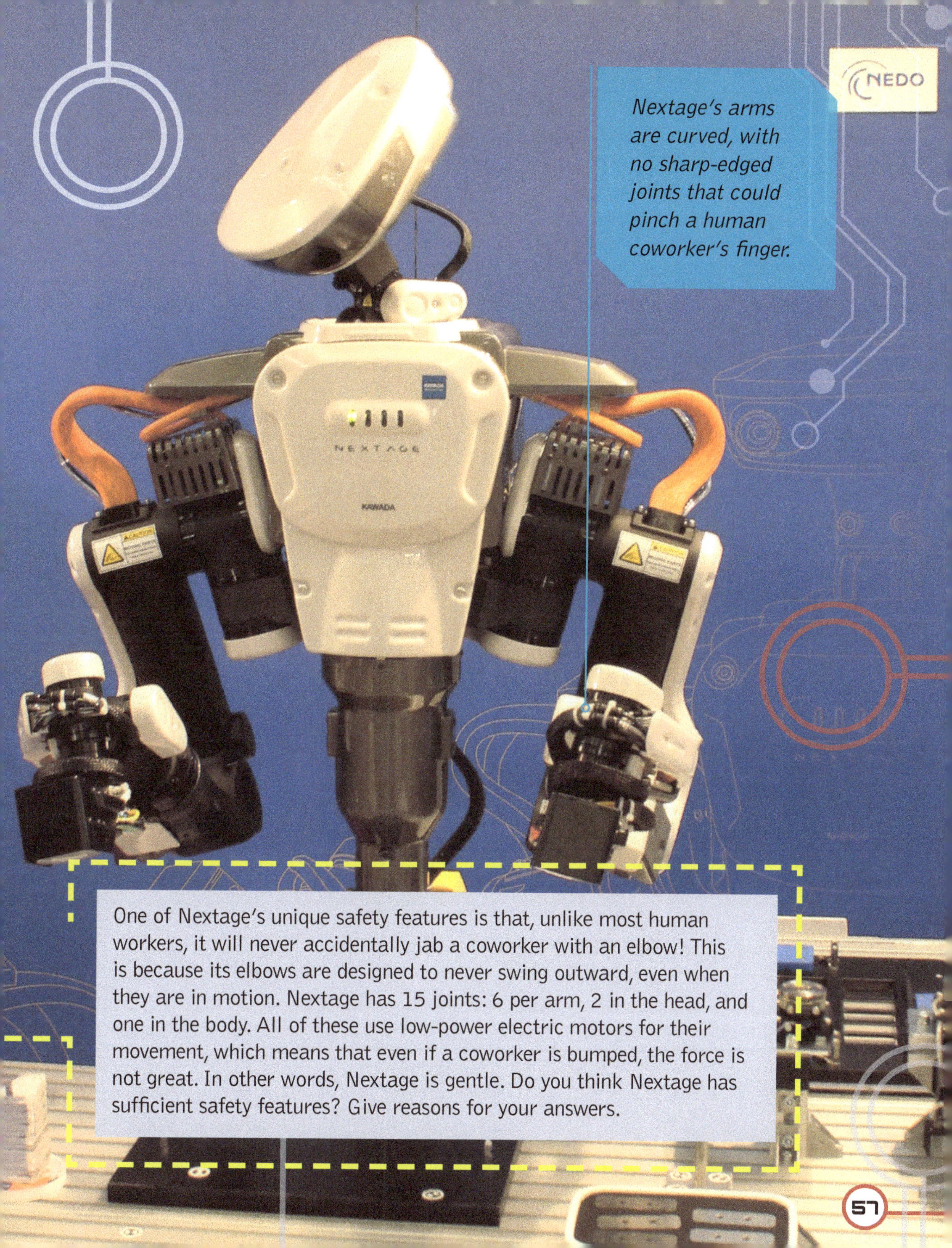

Nextage's arms are curved, with no sharp-edged joints that could pinch a human coworker's finger.

One of Nextage's unique safety features is that, unlike most human workers, it will never accidentally jab a coworker with an elbow! This is because its elbows are designed to never swing outward, even when they are in motion. Nextage has 15 joints: 6 per arm, 2 in the head, and one in the body. All of these use low-power electric motors for their movement, which means that even if a coworker is bumped, the force is not great. In other words, Nextage is gentle. Do you think Nextage has sufficient safety features? Give reasons for your answers.

Launched in 2014, Pepper is one of the newest generation of interactive humanoid robots. So far, Pepper has been employed as a greeter in banks and shops, and for taking food orders and payments in Pizza Hut restaurants across Asia. Its speakers enable Pepper to talk to customers, while a touchscreen lets the customer input their food order or find out information about products. Pepper is a mobile robot, but has few practical functions other than interaction with humans. To make this interaction pleasurable for the customer, Pepper has programming that gives it the ability to respond to the customer's emotions.

Communication

Humans communicate using not only words, but also tone of voice, head tilts, facial expressions, and gestures. Together, all these things reveal if we are happy, sad, nervous, angry, or surprised. Pepper responds to these emotions with appropriate words and phrases. In part, Pepper recognizes emotions through data received by cameras in its mouth and forehead. The information about the customer's face and posture—whether they are smiling, for example—is processed through the robot's computer. Pepper's microphones collect data about the customer's tone of voice. In addition, Pepper has touch sensors in its head and hands, so it knows when it has been touched. This means that Pepper has three of the five human senses: sight, hearing, and touch.

Pepper is also equipped and programmed to act in a human-like way. It has four microphones in its head, so when someone speaks to it, the robot identifies the direction of the sound and turns to face the customer. While Pepper speaks, it gestures with its hands and arms, as many humans do.

This Pepper is greeting a customer in an electronics store.

Pepper is on a mobile pedestal instead of legs, which makes the robot more stable.

ROBOT REVOLUTION

Pioneering, cloud-based robotics systems allow robots to benefit from huge amounts of computer power that their small bodies cannot hold. The "cloud" is simply a name for any group of powerful computers that can be accessed via the internet. Pepper is connected wirelessly to the internet. All the data that Pepper gathers from customers during its interactions is uploaded to a cloud-based artificial intelligence system. The data is processed in the cloud, and many of Pepper's spoken responses actually come from the cloud instead of from Pepper's onboard programming. There are a lot of different Peppers working all around the world, and all of them are uploading information to the cloud. This means that, as a group, the Peppers will "learn" to be better at interacting with people.

Robots are having a huge impact on many industries across the world. One workplace where they are becoming particularly popular is the classroom. Robots can become involved in education in three ways. First, they can help students learn to program a computer. You may yourself have programmed a basic "bot" to turn left and right. The second way that robots are finding their way into classrooms is through telepresence. Telepresence robots allow a teacher to teach a class without being in the same room. The teacher can speak and see through a robot in the classroom, interact with the class, take questions, and review work. This technology is already being adopted in some remote schools, as it allows teachers to give lessons without traveling a long distance. Students who are unable to attend school because of health problems can be taught at home using telepresence.

NAO

The third way in which robots are changing education is through fully autonomous humanoid robots. NAO is one of this pioneering generation of teaching robots. It can capture the attention of students, particularly those with learning difficulties. It can be programmed to take classes, concentrating for now on teaching life skills and communication. Like Pepper, NAO has three of the five human senses, so it reacts to a child's emotions, touches, and lapses in attention. NAO is also connected wirelessly to the cloud, so it can download appropriate responses, up-to-the-minute lessons, and "learn" from all the interactions that other NAOs are having with their students. NAO, like other robot pioneers, is paving the way for an exciting future in our industrial world!

The Alantim robot can give lectures and greet students.

So far, 10,000 NAOs have been sold around the world, costing around $8,000 each. The 23-in (58 cm) walking robot has two cameras, four microphones, two speakers, nine touch sensors, eight pressure sensors, and two infrared receivers and transmitters. Would you like to be taught by NAO? Would you prefer a telepresence teacher? Can you see any problems with robot teachers like this one?

artificial intelligence The ability of a machine to perform tasks that normally require human intelligence, like understanding speech.

autonomous Able to act independently.

compressed Squeezed or pressed.

digital Information or signals expressed as a pattern of 0s and 1s.

drones Driverless aircraft that can navigate independently.

electric motors Machines that change electrical energy into movement.

electronic circuits Loops around which electrical current can travel.

electronics Industry that develops and makes electrical devices such as computers.

empathy Ability to understand and share other people's feelings.

end effector The device at the end of a robotic arm.

exoskeleton External skeleton or covering.

Global Positioning System (GPS) A system that uses signals from satellites to determine a location.

herbicide A substance that kills plants.

hydraulic A system operated by moving and compressing liquid.

laser Intense beam of light.

manipulator Mechanical arm that can move things around.

manufacturing Making products using machinery and human labor.

near infrared light Light that humans cannot see.

odometry The use of motion sensors to calculate distance traveled.

optical fibers Thin strands through which light can travel.

pesticides Substances that kill insects or other animals that harm plants.

piston A solid rod that moves up and down inside a tube.

pneumatic A system operated by moving and compressing gas.

production lines Lines of machines or workers in a factory along which a product moves.

program A set of ordered instructions.

psychology Study of the human mind and behavior.

radiation A form of energy used in the treatment of cancer.

radio waves A form of energy that is used for sending invisible signals through the air.

sensors Devices that detect something and then react to it.

simulate Imitate the appearance of something.

stereovision Able to perceive three dimensions.

thermal imaging Using the heat given off by an object to produce an image of it.

transponders Devices for sending and receiving signals.

valve A device for controlling the movement of liquid or gas through a pipe.

voice synthesizers Devices that imitate speech.

wireless connection A link to a computer network, using radio waves instead of wires.

FOR MORE INFORMATION

Books

Ceceri, Kathy. *Robotics: Discover the Science and Technology of the Future with 20 Projects* (Build it Yourself). White River Junction, VT: Nomad Press, 2012.

Faust, Daniel R. *Flying Robots* (Robots and Robotics). New York, NY: PowerKids Press, 2016.

Freedman, Jeri. *Robots Through History* (Robotics Library). New York, NY: Rosen Central, 2011.

Mercer, Bobby. *The Robot Book: Build and Control 20 Electric Gizmos, Moving Machines, and Hacked Toys* (Science in Motion). Chicago, IL: Chicago Review Press, 2014.

Websites

Learn about robotics on the NASA website:
https://robotics.nasa.gov

Do some more research about different types of robots:
www.q-files.com/technology/electronics/robots

Take a closer look at robot technology:
www.explainthatstuff.com/robots.html

Play games and start new projects about robotics:
www.sciencekids.co.nz/robots.html

Publisher's note to educators and parents: Our editors have carefully reviewed these websites to ensure that they are suitable for students. Many websites change frequently, however, and we cannot guarantee that a site's future contents will continue to meet our high standards of quality and educational value. Be advised that students should be closely supervised whenever they access the Internet.